PASTOR OGHENETHOJA UMUTEME

UNDERSTAND WEALTH MAKING AND FINANCIAL PLANNING

PASTOR OGHENETHOJA UMUTEME

UNDERSTAND WEALTH MAKING AND FINANCIAL PLANNING

MEMOIRS
Cirencester

Published by Memoirs

MEMOIRS
PUBLISHING

Memoirs Books

1A The Wool Market, Cirencester, Gloucestershire, GL7 2PR
info@memoirsbooks.co.uk | www.memoirspublishing.com

Understand Wealth Making and Financial Planning

First published in England, 2015

ISBN 978-1-909874-83-1

Address all enquiries to the publisher; Restoration Media House Limited
+234-8101700665, +2348076190064, Email: rmhltd.info@gmail.com

Printed in England

DEDICATION

To my wife, Adokiye Obele Umuteme -
A love to behold, and a trust to keep

CONTENTS

	Introduction	
Chapter 1	How The Altar Influences Wealth Making	Page 1
Chapter 2	Sustaining Wealth	Page 27
Chapter 3	Making Wealth the Right Way	Page 45
Chapter 4	Why Plan Your Money?	Page 56
Chapter 5	Financial Planning Thoughts	Page 68
Chapter 6	Effect of Lack of Financial Planning	Page 76
Chapter 7	The Spirit of Financial Planning	Page 85
Chapter 8	The Character of a Financial Planner	Page 102
Chapter 9	The Enemies of Financial Planning	Page 109
Chapter 10	Wisdom for Investment	Page 124
Chapter 11	Stages of Financial Planning	Page 142
Chapter 12	Too Much Money	Page 154
Chapter 13	Striving During Famine	Page 167
Chapter 14	Save Your Tomorrow Today	Page 179
	Covenant Confession	Page 182
	Books by the same author	Page 183
	About the author	Page 184
	References	Page 187

INTRODUCTION

This book may not make any sense to anyone having the spirit of covetousness. That has to be dealt with first, because the spirit of covetousness is the spirit of poverty and greed. If you see yourself always imagining how much money your neighbour is worth, then you are a covetous person. If you are the type who always believes that someone has to give you money because you saw them with money, then you are on your way to poverty and this book may not make sense to you.

My life underwent a transformation the day I came across Jeremiah 17:5-8: *'Thus saith the Lord; Cursed be the man that trusteth in man, and maketh flesh his arm, and whose heart departeth from the Lord. For he shall be like the heath in the desert, and shall not see when good cometh; but shall inhabit the parched places in the wilderness, in a salt land and not inhabited. Blessed is the man that trusteth in the Lord, and whose hope the Lord is. For he shall be as a tree planted by the waters, and that spreadeth out her roots by the river, and shall not see when heat cometh, but her leaf shall be green; and shall not be careful in the year of drought, neither shall cease from yielding fruit',* and I began to see the reason why depending on our fellow men will bring our downfall. Those who put their trust in their fellow men to help them are under the curse in that passage of the Bible and shall not see when good opportunities come their way, while those who trust in the Lord to provide for them are waxing great and strong daily as a tree planted by the river side, with evergreen leaves, and will not cease from bearing fruits. With this, our attention is now unto the Lord in heaven, and as we serve Him, He will provide us with our hearts' desires. Abraham recounted this when he said that God would surely provide in His mount – Genesis 22:14. We knew that Abraham lived a life of altar worship, and that every time he went to worship the Lord, He always provided for His upkeep. The same reason Jesus says our God can provide in abundance for us.

This book is a revelation of the truth, and nothing but the truth. It is set in three stages – how the Altar helps in the acquisition of wealth, how to plan your money and then how invest for tomorrow. It is a book many have requested me to write on how to overcome the fangs of famine.

Like the Biblical Prophet Agabus, the Spirit has informed me that there will be great famine from August 2017 through 2027. By 2028 the Lord will have a perfect church that will serve and worship His glorious reign. In the days of Agabus his prophecy came to pass as revealed in the days of Claudius Caesar - Acts *11:28: And there stood up one of them named Agabus, and signified by the Spirit that there should be great dearth throughout all the world: which came to pass in the days of Claudius Caesar.*

With worldwide famine imminent, it is necessary that the children of God be taught the principle of creating wealth and financial planning. Now you will know how to make and spend more authentic money through understanding the secrets of financial planning.

Is making money a sin? No - I don't ever think so. Can we live without money? I don't think that either. But the Bible says that the love of money is the root of all evil - that is it! Giving all your heart to the chasing of money will make you have evil thoughts because of lack of patience.

Money is not evil on its own. The Bible says in Proverbs 10:22 that the blessings of the Lord make us rich and add no sorrow to it. With wisdom, we would learn how to make money, spend it wisely and have time for God, instead of being too busy chasing after it and forsaking God, and then heading for hell – Proverbs 15:24: *The way of life is above to the wise, that he may depart from hell beneath.*

If you don't plan your money, the money will plan you. Before you cross a river, try to find out what is there – either there are crocodiles or other wild river creatures - so when you swim or use a boat across you shouldn't be taken unawares. You cannot be in a river that is flowing and begging for water to drink, and in the same way, we cannot be filled with the Holy Spirit and lack the wisdom to make ends meet.

The Bible taught us that the love of money is the root of every evil – 1 Timothy 6:10. It equally says, of what use will it be for someone to gain the whole world and lose his soul? – Matthew 16:26. In the midst of these, God still wants His children to live above want daily. But to do this, we are implored to seek after righteousness. Hence the Bible says (1 Timothy 6:11-12): *But thou, O man of God, flee these things; and follow after righteousness, godliness, faith, love, patience, meekness. Fight the good fight of faith, lay hold on eternal life, whereunto thou art also called, and hast professed a good profession before many witnesses.* This is the premise on which I write this book, so that as children of God, we may be guided on what to do, and we may be seen as fighting the good fight of faith in all our human endeavours so that even in business we may be sincere and prudent. We won't be seen wasting resources, and our barns will not be empty in time of famine.

A time came when Jesus also said we should not worry over the things the world worries about, since we could not count the strands of hair on our head – Luke 12:7: *But even the very hairs of your head are all numbered. Fear not therefore: ye are of more value than many sparrows.*

The spirit of wealth making and finance planning comes as we mature in the things of the Lord. This is why Jesus says the good things of the world are added unto us when we love the Lord; they aren't the main reward for walking with God. This however is what many see as a difficult path to tread – walking before the statutes of the Lord.

Life is not about marrying; it is about staying married. It is also not about getting a job; it is about staying in the job. So also is wealth – it is how to sustain it that really matters, in such a way that we are not worn out.

Many companies worldwide say that one can go on retirement at age 45 or after 15 years of service in the company. The truth is, many still work to age 60 and find it difficult to accept the reality of retiring. Many have reduced their ages over time to ensure they are still within the employable age. Why? It is the fear that lack of money brings to the heart. Should we then become liars in order to put food on our tables? What happens to our souls if we toe the path of insincerity? This is the reason for this book.

I had a job, and for two years I could hardly account for my salary. I knew I did spent it on something, but what it was spent on, I couldn't tell. My wife and I sat down through the night of that discovery to plan our lives. That was when my financial tutelage began. First I looked at all sources of waste, and started cutting them out. I thought of what could keep me busy when I retired from work. I also started thinking about early retirement.

Back then I never had a clue that I would be called into God's vineyard someday, though I loved pastors and admired their work in that vineyard. But after that self-discovery I made another blunder, and this was taking loans for personal effects. Some of my colleagues went into stock trading because it was yielding more returns, but a few years down the line, it made them debtors too.

Many have been reading books on financial management. I was also a fervent visitor to the Investopedia website[1], where I was also learning about finance management. I encouraged my wife to visit the website often. Our wastage habit greatly reduced as we became financially informed. We had our home within our financial reach and we were happy and managing money. We thought of investment opportunities that we could invest in, and while we were doing that, the call came and we found ourselves in the vineyard of God. The Lord made us see the gifts in our lives and I started writing books with much vigour. Even with all the discouragement I received, the Lord strengthened me to move forward, and this is one of the

[1] www.investopedia.com

'wisdom-in-books' that you are reading. This is my fifteenth published book since my first in November 2009.

In this book, we will be discussing our financial needs as we grow in life, depending on the work we chose and how we intend to live our lives. If we have a working financial plan, we will have enough time to serve God. People find it difficult to serve God because they have involved themselves in unnecessary financial hiccups. Poor financial planning makes us serve mammon and have less or no time for God.

The government employs economic austerity measures to save the nation from heading down the pan during financial crisis. Many nations are suffering financial handicap because no one was ever taught how to manage money as a child.

Firstly, a look at our homes, church and society. One thing is common, and that is waste. One question that would come into our hearts is why these wastes were generated, and who did it. Many of us will argue that waste is part of our living, but I would want to express my concern over what I would term non-essential waste. Financial planning aims at eliminating non-essential waste. I have worked in the same establishment as some women, earning the same salaries as them. But while I could see the use of my income, obviously most of them have wasted the same income in worthless sightseeing travels and the buying of fashion items. This is what pushed my quest into financial planning.

Another reason why I am in this discourse is because I have seen companies say that their employees can actually go on early retirement from the age of 45 as mentioned earlier. Why then are people working till they are old? Some have reduced their declared age over the years to ensure they are still within the employment age – why? The answer is lack of financial planning.

Thirdly, the pursuit of money has made many idol worshippers who have no time for God. I have seen primary school teachers with meagre salaries training children to become successful graduates in Nigeria, while in the same vein, I have seen children of millionaires becoming wayward in society, and these millionaires dying wretched as banks come after their estates when they die. Why? Again, it is lack of financial planning.

Right from my secondary school days as I was being taught economics, my concern has been cost savings. In engineering management, I understood that engineering is about Cost, Time and Resource (CTR) measurement. Engineers calculate design life and all that, to help in the financial planning of the next cycle of capital projects. As a pastor in God's vineyard over the years in counselling young people, I have come to know that poor financial planning skills is why many have become financially stagnant, while many acclaimed spiritual churches turn their minds to believing in all manner of spiritual attacks as the basis for not able to meet their financial obligations. While I am not against that belief because it does happen, most financial hiccups are caused by lack of discipline in money spending. In the first two years of my employment, it was difficult for me to actually point at what I spent my income on, as I mentioned. It wasn't a spiritual attack; it was a delinquent attitude in me. How will a woman manage her home, as explained in Proverbs 14:1: *'Every wise woman buildeth her house: but the foolish plucketh it down with her hands*', if she is not trained in wealth creation and financial planning principles?

This book is an invaluable resource that will not only help many to become judicious in financial matters, but will also let us know that making wealth is not sin after all provided, we can still keep our souls from lusting after the devil. I encourage you to have a notebook and pen by your side to put down the wisdom that will spring out of the book as you read on.

Pst. Oghenethoja Umuteme
Royal Diamonds Int'l Church
(aka Christ Movement)
Port Harcourt, Nigeria

CHAPTER ONE

HOW THE ALTAR INFLUENCES WEALTH MAKING

Anyone desiring wealth would be interested in what the Lord says is the source of wealth. In His several teachings where He made reference to wealth, one statement stands out and that verse is Matthew 6:33: *But seek ye first the kingdom of God, and his righteousness; and all these things shall be added unto you.* We will now ponder this verse of the Bible so as to suck honey from it.

The last line there says that wealth is an addition unto us – more like a reward for our faithfulness to the Lord. A striking statement is also found in verse 34: *Take therefore no thought for the morrow: for the morrow shall take thought for the things of itself. Sufficient unto the day is the evil thereof.* To make wealth, one needs to ponder over this last verse, and as we do we will find that wealth does not come through hustling and bustling. Some advice is given in Proverbs 23:4: *Labour not to be rich: cease from thine own wisdom.* Another passage in the Bible that also explains to us that God is the only one who provides wealth is found in Deuteronomy 8:7-10: *For the Lord thy God bringeth thee into a good land, a land of brooks of water, of fountains and depths that spring out of valleys and hills; A land of wheat, and barley, and vines, and fig trees, and pomegranates; a land of oil olive, and honey; A land wherein thou shalt eat bread without scarceness, thou shalt not lack any thing in it; a land whose stones are iron, and out of whose hills thou mayest dig brass. When thou hast eaten and art full, then thou shalt bless the Lord thy God for the good land which he hath given thee.*

In the light of the above statement from God to the Israelites, we can see that He made them to know ahead of time the wealth that lies in wait for them in the land – agricultural produce, plenty of iron and brass. With these they can venture into food processing and mining. There is so much in the land waiting for your exploration and exploitation, provided you are willing to learn His ways and obedient to put the wisdom into practice. Remember too that the Garden of Eden was filled with wealth – Genesis 2:10-12: *And a river went out of Eden to water the garden; and from thence it was parted, and became into four heads. The name of the first is Pison: that is it which compasseth the whole land of Havilah, where there is gold; And the gold of that land is good: there is bdellium and the onyx stone.*

Taking the instruction from Genesis 1:26 that we should have dominion, it is expected that Adam should have explored the river to fish in it, and also mine the minerals that were in the land. But before all these could happen, sin took him out of the garden.

You don't have to struggle to make wealth; it comes through obedience to the instructions from the realm of the spirit, because the wealth of this world is held in spiritual high places. This is why Jacob also, knowing that God is the only one who can give wealth, vowed in Genesis 28:20-22: ... *saying, If God will be with me, and will keep me in this way that I go, and will give me bread to eat, and raiment to put on, So that I come again to my father's house in peace; then shall the Lord be my God: And this stone, which I have set for a pillar, shall be God's house:*

and of all that thou shalt give me I will surely give the tenth unto thee. Jacob was hopeful that he would be wealthy hence he said, '*of all that thou shalt give me.*' Jacob knew that the Lord could bless him in abundance, hence on another occasion after wrestling with the Lord to the extent of risking an injury that made him limp all through his life, he demanded that he must be blessed and there he got his desire (Genesis 32:24-29).

How do we seek God? Let's take learning from Genesis 13:4: *Unto the place of the altar, which he had made there at the first: and there Abram called on the name of the Lord.* Did Abraham only call on the name of the Lord all the days of his life? No! He sacrificed on the Altar unto the Lord to the extent that he did not even withhold his son from the Lord when God demanded that the son should be sacrificed – so the Lord handed over unto Abraham a covenant of blessings, protection, and preservation of life – Genesis 22:15-17: *And the angel of the Lord called unto Abraham out of heaven the second time, And said, By myself have I sworn, saith the Lord, for because thou hast done this thing, and hast not withheld thy son, thine only son: That in blessing I will bless thee, and in multiplying I will multiply thy seed as the stars of the heaven, and as the sand which is upon the sea shore;*

and thy seed shall possess the gate of his enemies. And Abraham became wealthy hereafter. We can also take learning from Psalms 28:2: *Hear the voice of my supplications, when I cry unto thee, when I lift up my hands toward thy holy oracle.* Here, David cried unto God, lifting up his hands towards the Lord's holy oracle.

In revealing the source of Solomon's great wealth, the Bible says (1 Kings 3:3-4): *And Solomon loved the Lord … a thousand burnt offerings did Solomon offer upon that altar.* And later, the altar spoke in his favour – God remembered his sacrifice upon the altar and appeared to him in a dream, giving him a 'blank cheque' request, and though Solomon only asked for wisdom, God also gave him riches. That altar which bears the sacrifices of Solomon was in the tabernacle built by Moses which lies in Mount Gibeon (1 Chronicles 21:29), a mountain over which the sun stood still when Joshua and his soldiers fought to posses the land of Canaan. The testimony of victory over this mount is enough for every wise and God-fearing individual to seek the face of the Lord with a sacrifice that will move Him. This is why, when people are giving testimonies of the great work the Lord did for them when they pray before the altar, anyone who is wise will quickly sow a sacrificial seed upon the altar.

This is the wisdom here from what we get from Solomon's sacrifice of seeking right judgement, and the addition of influence and affluence by God.

What am I trying to say here? That wealth comes only from the Lord, and it has to do with our dedication to service at His altar. A secret is also revealed in the book of Proverbs 23:5, which says: ...for riches *certainly make themselves wings; they fly away as an eagle toward heaven.* Riches fly towards where? Heaven, of course! Heaven is made up of spiritual realms – we have the lower heaven, the middle and the upper heaven. Every wealth on earth is harnessed with the power from heaven, either from the devil or God, and so if we would submit to Jesus who has all powers in His hand (Matthew 28:18), we will become rich as long as we obey His commands, and the day we disobey, the riches will fly away to where they came from. This is why they do not last from one generation to the next. When the Lord called me He said to me – 'if you see yourself struggling, then you are about to fail.' I will want us to take this to heart – wealth comes through obedience to the instructions of God.

Some believers have wondered why they can't make ends meet yet. Many have also thought that the moment they give their life to Christ, all things will just work out in their favour. I have also heard many believers challenging God to make things happen in their favour because they pay their tithes. They have read through the pages of the Bible hoping to get out of 'want.' They have prayed, they have asked, but it seems that the cloud is not lifting for their requests to pass through.

The truth is that there is more to it. There is more that that man standing behind the pulpit can do for you in this wealth-seeking regard. This is a firm truth and a secret. As a priest, he ministers before the Lord, the anointed of God, Jesus Christ who establishes him with divine wealth-making secrets that will make him stand firm in defence of the truth.

We would be taking learning from 1 Samuel 2:35-36: *And I will raise me up a faithful priest, that shall do according to that which is in mine heart and in my mind: and I will build him a sure house; and he shall walk before mine anointed for ever. And it shall come to pass, that every one that is left in thine house shall come and crouch to him for a piece of silver and a morsel of bread, and shall say, Put me, I pray thee, into one of the priests 'offices, that I may eat a piece of bread.* Samuel was raised after the heart of God to walk before the Lord and he indeed excelled according to the promise of God to build him a sure house, as we have read. The only way others who are out of the priestly ordinances will eat will be to meet Samuel to appoint them so that they will also minister at the altar to be able to eat bread. If you want wealth, you must support the priest of the Lord in your midst, as it is pleasing unto the Lord. Eli's children were greedy and the Lord took them out of His altar.

Some have used the Bible passage of 1 Peter 2:9 to say that we are all now qualified to offer priestly oblation before the Lord. We will now see this portion together - *But ye are a chosen generation, a royal priesthood, an holy nation, a peculiar people; that ye should shew forth the praises of him who hath called you out of darkness into his marvellous light.* What we just read talks about God making a choice, which will now make us become His chosen. If everyone can offer oblation unto Him, then there is no need for a choice, which after obtaining mercy, is appointed to officiate before the ensign of heavenly things made physical. In line with the raising of Samuel, Peter's conversation can be seen as one directed at specially selected choice-people whom God will reveal secrets to that will make them function as a royal priesthood, holy nation and peculiar people who would always show forth the praise and the testimony of the Lord. And if you are convinced that the man behind the pulpit does not have the anointing to make things happen, then pray that the Lord should lead you to one of His own. Don't forget that the devil also has his own, who also stand behind the pulpit.

Have this at the back of your mind – that wealth making starts from the altar, and the wisdom for financial planning resides in the immortal realm, and will be released as oracles unto you whenever you seek it: Psalm 28:1-2: *Unto thee will I cry, O Lord my rock; be not silent to me: lest, if thou be silent to me, I become like them that go down into the pit. Hear the voice of my supplications, when I cry unto thee, when I lift up my hands toward thy holy oracle.*

If you want wealth, you need an altar raised by the arm of the Lord in your midst. This arm must empower you spiritually with the anointing he bears to also raise an altar linked to the one he has raised, and from that altar you can make your prayers. We learnt that the Egyptians' midwives became wealthy because they preserved what belong to God – His chosen people – Exodus 1:20-21: *Therefore God dealt well with the midwives: and the people multiplied, and waxed very mighty. And it came to pass, because the midwives feared God, that he made them houses.* Can we see that?

The learning here is that if we can defend the work of the Lord by preserving His chosen and 'anointed-in-covenant' with Him, He is faithful to reward us. Jesus referred to the reward accompanying this gesture too when He said (Matthew 10:40-42): *He that receiveth you receiveth me, and he that receiveth me receiveth him that sent me. He that receiveth a prophet in the name of a prophet shall receive a prophet's reward; and he that receiveth a righteous man in the name of a righteous man shall receive a righteous man's reward. And whosoever shall give to drink unto one of these little ones a cup of cold water only in the name of a disciple, verily I say unto you, he shall in no wise lose his reward.* Someone has been chosen to officiate at the altar of the Lord, your duty is to look after him in your material things, while he stretches the anointing towards you. Don't forget that a servant of God walks before the Anointed, the Christ, and the angels follows the Anointed wherever he leads, and so whatever regard you give to God's servant as an appreciation for the work of the Lord he is doing shall never go unrecognised. The angels who are ministering to the Lord will definitely mark you for divine favour. These angels will fulfil your heart's desire just as one provided food for Elijah in 1 Kings 19, on his way to the mountain of the Lord.

The Lord yearns for humble and loyal people who He will bless, a learning we can get from Abraham's life – Genesis 23:7: *And Abraham stood up, and bowed himself to the people of the land, even to the children of Heth*. He bowed down before those he lived in their midst who had referred to him as a mighty prince in verse 6: *Hear us, my lord: thou art a mighty prince among us*. Humility and loyalty precedes wealth making – Proverbs 13:7: *There is that maketh himself rich, yet hath nothing: there is that maketh himself poor, yet hath great riches.*

We would take learning also from the story of Job, when his friends came to advise him, and while it seems as though they were sympathising with his condition as the Lord had allowed the devil to take away his carnal possessions and also dealt with his flesh, God saw it as a mockery of His person. And later, for them to be saved, God ordered that they take a sacrifice to His servant Job, who would pray for them, and then the Lord used their obedience to rain blessings upon Job, and them – Job 42:6: *And it was so, that after the Lord had spoken these words unto Job, the Lord said to Eliphaz the Temanite, My wrath is kindled against thee, and against thy two friends:*

for ye have not spoken of me the thing that is right, as my servant Job hath. Therefore take unto you now seven bullocks and seven rams, and go to my servant Job, and offer up for yourselves a burnt offering; and my servant Job shall pray for you: for him will I accept: lest I deal with you after your folly, in that ye have not spoken of me the thing which is right, like my servant Job. So Eliphaz the Temanite and Bildad the Shuhite and Zophar the Naamathite went, and did according as the Lord commanded them: the Lord also accepted Job. And the Lord turned the captivity of Job, when he prayed for his friends: also the Lord gave Job twice as much as he had before. This tells us why Job was so rich before his predicament, which was a test of faith, because the Lord was trying to make him whiter – Daniel 11:35: *And some of them of understanding shall fall, to try them, and to purge, and to make them white…* I would advise that we should be careful of what we say when we see a torn in the flesh of servants of God, so that we wouldn't incur God's wrath.

The servant of God needs to offer prayers on your behalf, and that would turn the eyes of the Lord to you. The Prophet Samuel made reference to this onerous duty of the servant of God when he said in 1 Samuel 12:23:

Moreover as for me, God forbid that I should sin against the Lord in ceasing to pray for you: but I will teach you the good and the right way. I would advise that if you want the increase of the Lord, learn to keep the man behind the pulpit on duty. He shouldn't be thinking of how to fend for himself, and you expect him to still be behind the altar to pray for you. Despite the apostles' relationship with Jesus, they still needed Peter to minister the Holy Spirit. Take the words of Isaiah 50:10-11 to heart – those who fail to obey the instructions from God's servants end up in sorrow: *Who is among you that feareth the Lord, that obeyeth the voice of his servant,* that *walketh in darkness, and hath no light? let him trust in the name of the Lord, and stay upon his God. Behold, all ye that kindle a fire, that compass yourselves about with sparks: walk in the light of your fire, and in the sparks that ye have kindled. This shall ye have of mine hand; ye shall lie down in sorrow.* The altar needs your sacrifices, offerings and tithes as a means of inhcriting thc good of the land. It all boils down to willingness and obedience – Isaiah 1:19: *If ye be willing and obedient, ye shall eat the good of the land.*

Another special seed is prophetic seed. Sowing into the life of a servant of God, provided he is a fertile land, call of the Lord, will yield the kind of increase that will amaze you. In 1 Thessalonians 5:12-13, Saint Paul implored the church to take proper care of the servants of God who bear rule over them - *And we beseech you, brethren, to know them which labour among you, and are over you in the Lord, and admonish you; And to esteem them very highly in love for their work's sake.* You can see the use of the words *esteem them very highly in love,* used to express your obligation for those who stand on the altar to ensure you break through on every side.

There is no wealth without obedience to the service of an altar. The moment an altar is raised in a land, the land and all that is in it is taken over by the Lord and handed over to the one who raised the altar according to the covenant of relationship between him and God. And angels are deployed to fence the wealth of the land and are then, at the command of the Lord, at will to take whatever is in the land and hand over to anyone who is faithful to the call of the altar. A portion of the Bible that will explain this to you is Genesis 13:17: *Arise, walk through the land in the length of it and in the breadth of it; for I will give it unto thee.* Abraham had possessed the land with the several altars he had raised, because the Lord was with him. It is just common sense that anyone who would live and prosper in the land would get it from

Abraham, and for this to happen, such a person must be at peace with Abraham.

When the Lord calls His servants, he apportions unto them territories, where they have influence and control over every spiritual power and the wealth situated within the clouded territory. This is how God takes over the kingdoms of the earth and hands them over to custodians, who we call the servants of God – Revelation 11:15: *And the seventh angel sounded; and there were great voices in heaven, saying, The kingdoms of this world are become the kingdoms of our Lord, and of his Christ; and he shall reign for ever and ever.* Be it also known here that you do not pay your tithes and offerings in any altar you see if you want to be rich without experiencing sorrows (Proverbs 10:22); you should take it to the altar of the Lord that controls the territory where your source of income is located, then you will be favoured – 2 Chronicles 31:10: *Since the people began to bring the offerings into the house of the Lord, we have had enough to eat, and have left plenty: for the Lord hath blessed his people; and that which is left is this great store.* When God spoke to Abraham about sacrificing his only Son, Isaac, He told him that it must be done on a mountain that He would show Abraham – Genesis 22:2: *And he said, Take now thy son, thine only son, whom thou lovest, even Isaac, and get thee into the land of Moriah. And offer him there for a burnt- offering upon one of the mountains which I will tell thee of.* If Abraham had decided to do that outside where God was showing him, he would have committed murder, and wouldn't have seen the replacement *ram caught in the thicket by his horns.* If we do our sacrifices unto the Lord as He directs then we would be blessed with His provision – Genesis 22:14: *And Abraham called the name of that place Jehovah- jireh. As it is said to this day,* '**In the mount of Jehovah it shall be provided**.' Can you see that? Our provisions are waiting for us in His mount – right at the altar where you make your sacrifices. Do you seek wealth? It is waiting for you at the altar according to the measure of your freewill sacrifices. We can infer from Matthew 25:15: *...to every man according to his several ability*, that God gives us talents according to our walk with Him, because your ability is displayed in your faith. And your faith is a measure of what you would sacrifice unto the Lord.

The widow giving her two last mites (Luke 21:2-3) is a clear example of this fact of life, that we give the amount we give as sacrifices out of our faith. The widow got the recommendation of the Lord because she gave her all –

Luke 21:3: … *Of a truth I say unto you, that this poor widow hath cast in more than they all … but she of her penury hath cast in all the living that she had.* Penury means poverty, yet she gave, and the Lord didn't stop her from doing so because she was poor. Everybody must give an offering to the Lord whenever we are in His temple to worship Him. Our offerings and tithes are instruments of worship and total dependence on God. The altar returns to you in good measures, pressed down and shaken together, whatever you offered on the altar as a mark of appreciation. If man gives his time to his wife and adorns her with ornaments of beauty, the smile that comes from her as a result of this is an appreciation that the husband won't forget in a hurry. If you want wealth, your obedience to the call of the altar is non-negotiable.

And this understanding may have prompted David to say (1 Chronicles 21:24) … *but I will verily buy it for the full price: for I will not take that which is thine for the Lord, nor offer burnt offerings without cost.* Before David would do this, he was commanded by the Lord through His prophet Gad - 1 Chronicles 21:18: *Then the angel of the Lord commanded Gad to say to David, that David should go up, and set up an altar unto the Lord in the threshing floor of Ornan the Jebusite.* And we are told that

David obeyed to set up the altar –1 Chronicles 21:19: *And David went up at the saying of Gad, which he spake in the name of the Lord.*

David feared God and the result is what we just read. Do you fear God? Many times I have heard people grumble when told by servants of God to makes releases, and they would say they are waiting for the Lord to speak to them. The learning we get here is that God can decide to speak to His servants as He did to Gad instead of David, and He expects that we fulfil the request. If God also senses pride in someone, He wouldn't speak to such a person. David indeed spoke to God and He heard him as recorded in verse 17. It was after this that God spoke to Gad. Why didn't He speak to David, who entreated the Lord to withdraw His sword? The learning is that after we had prayed, the Lord can mention your case to His servants and you may be requested to make a release.

When Jesus met Zacchaeus, the first thing He mentioned was dining in his house – that is a request for a release. When He sent His disciples out to get the donkey on which He rode into Jerusalem, He expected the owner to grant the release. If you truly love the Lord and do appreciate all He has done for you, expect that one day He will request a release from your hand. If the little boy can offer his five loaves of bread and two fishes at the request of Jesus in John 6:9, what are you waiting for to make that release when the Lord needs it?

Though the Bible didn't go further to say what happened to the twelve baskets of the fragments of the bread that were gathered, it is obvious that they were given to the lad, because after then Jesus departed from them and the disciples also went looking for Him. If they were in possession of the breads, the crowd would have followed them immediately. The fact that the crowd only returned the following day proves this point. And when they wanted to know what to do to show that they were doing the work of God, this is what ensued – John 6:28-29: *Then said they unto him, What shall we do, that we might work the works of God? Jesus answered and said unto them, This is the work of God, that ye believe on him whom he hath sent.* And instead of doing what He commanded, they were looking for a sign. Are these people who want to live abundant life? Jesus didn't say that they should believe in Him alone, but to believe whoever comes in the name of the Lord, because very soon He was going to leave and then would be raising men to do His work. And indeed just as today, the people wanted signs and wonders, despite the multiplication of the five loaves of bread and two fishes they had seen the previous day. It is people with this kind of thinking that the devil deceives daily with petty miracles and then locks their souls in total darkness, where they do not find help, but keep on struggling to make ends meet.

How do you know that the Lord is blessing you through His servant? It is by observation and confirmation. Laban, Jacob's inlaw knew this – Genesis 30:27: ... *for I have learned by experience that the Lord hath blessed me for thy sake.* And for this Laban said in verse 28 - *And he said, 'appoint me thy wages, and I will give it.'* It is only right that one good turn should deserve another. What do you think is the wages of the servant of God for all that the Lord has blessed you with through the anointing upon him? Will it be fair that he labours to seek that which you have in abundance?

What we have said so far places a demand of humility, loyalty and submission from us to the vision the servant of God drives for the Lord. If you will obey him, you shall be even as glad as the widow in 1 Kings 17:15,16: *And she went and did according to the saying of Elijah: and she, and he, and her house, did eat many days. And the barrel of meal wasted not, neither did the cruse of oil fail, according to the word of the Lord, which he spake by Elijah.* Before this happened to her, she had given her last morsel of bread to the servant of God. In some cases, before a release is made in your favour from the immortal realm of the Lord, he is informed, and in some cases he can stop the release from happening by making a strong case against you which the realm would adjudge a righteous case, then you may be informed in your dream to go and make peace with him. Once that is done, he lifts the barrier, and you would have your release.

When I discovered that my congregation didn't understand how disobedience to the instructions of a servant of God is treated as an act of disloyalty to the course of the realm to take this world from the control of the devil and would attract serious penalty of denial, I stopped making announcements requiring their dedication, until I had taught it, so that their nonchalant attitude of negligence due to their spiritual ignorance is not taken against them.

Some time in 2011, I heard – 'teach them how to release for the work you are doing in the Lord, else they won't receive increase.'

You are now reading a guided secret that have been enjoyed by few – Matthew 7:14: *Because strait is the gate, and narrow is the way, which leadeth unto life, and few there be that find it*, but open your heart as you read on, and if you put what is here to practice, you will not only make wealth, but you won't lose your soul to the devil. I have prayed and sought this from the immortal realm of spiritual consciousness, why many suffer without the ability to make ends meet despite their prayers. Confessing Jesus as your Lord and Saviour has helped to pay the debt of sin and eternal condemnation that was hanging round your neck before you repented. Now that you have salvation, you need now to follow Him wherever He leads, and He is going to lead you into the hands of one of His servants, where He is sure you will be taken through the culture of the Kingdom, and to be able to live on Earth, enjoying the abundance of this Earth in a manner that will not make you lose your soul to the devil's antics. Jesus expects you to have wisdom to understand Him and apply His teaching wherever you will be. He taught in the open using the wisdom and terminologies of various professions, and He expects His audience to get His message and make meaning out of it. This explains that He expects us to have a profession.

For every good life you admire, there are prices to pay – education, planning, sleepless nights, meeting people and accepting them, etc. Your reasoning must transcend cultural and traditional boundaries. The kind of lifestyle of many believers is not fit for evangelism, nor to talk of the kind of life that would make wealth.

Why am I talking about wealth? Many have disturbed me as they cry about not being favoured by the Lord. Some have accused me, saying that the lines are only falling for me in pleasant places. I have wanted to concentrate on the message of Salvation only, but many want to make wealth, and the crusades too need money, so it would be right to teach the children of God the right way to make wealth, so that the 'curiosity that kills the cat' won't take them out of heaven.

Here, at last, is the secret to making wealth. There is a price to pay – on top of this is humility and loyalty to the course of God in the life of any of His servant whom you have decided to submit under. This servant also has a lot to do in ensuring that your soul is led to a resting place in the bosom of the Lord.

To this end, I would want us to have a deeper look into the words in Mark 10:29-30: *Truly, I say to you, there is no one who has left house or brothers or sisters or mother or father or children or lands, for my sake and for the gospel. Who will not receive a hundredfold now in this time, houses and brothers and sisters and mothers and children and lands, with persecutions, and in the age to come eternal life.* The more I meditate on this portion of the Bible, the more life explains itself to me. From Jesus' statement we can get all we need if we choose to, though with caution – persecutions! What we should be careful about is not to lose our soul – we must determine to make heaven, and live in the glory of the Father. A further analysis of His word in that portion of the book of Mark we just read would show that He hasn't really advised that we should go after material things.

Now people have asked me why would there be *persecutions*, if one follows the Lord, and still desire to have all the beautiful things of life - *houses and brothers and sisters and mothers and children and lands*? Before we would answer this, let's also take a look at Proverbs 19:4,7: *Wealth maketh many friends; but the poor is separated from his neighbour. All the brethren of the poor do hate him...* We would then infer from this wisdom that anyone who would get all that the Lord spoke about in the book of Mark, we read earlier is one experiencing great wealth. So Christ referred to whoever will leave all to follow Him as one with the capacity to make great wealth. It wouldn't be any wonder then why many servants of God who desire wealth have really amassed wealth, and have been the talk on people's lips, and many have often been angry about why a servant of God should be so wealthy. The concern then is the word 'persecutions', used earlier in Mark 10:30. Where will the persecutions come from? The truth is that whatever we desire in this Earth is in the hand of the devil. The devil is in the seat of power; hence unrighteousness has taken over the world – Ephesians 6:12. The devil, through one of his demons – mammon - has also taken over the wealth of the nations. Borrowing a clue from the temptation of Jesus – Matthew 4:8-9: *Again, the devil taketh him up into an exceeding high mountain, and sheweth him all the kingdoms of the world, and the glory of them; And saith unto him, All these things will I give thee, if thou wilt fall down and worship me*, we would see that the devil has hold of everything in the world except power. So with the Power of the Lord (Matthew 28:18), we can command the devil around, and get our wealth released from whoever is in possession of it – Isaiah 61:6. This is only when we would have enough resources – money and materials, *And we shall build the old wastes, we shall raise up the former desolations, and we shall repair the waste cities, the desolations of many generations*

– Isaiah 61:4. This brief exploration explains why many are unable to make ends meet even after confessing Jesus as their Lord and Saviour, because they haven't receive the Power that controls things here on Earth.

CHAPTER TWO

SUSTAINING WEALTH

It is not about making money and wealth; it is also about having the power to sustain them. You cannot sustain your wealth until you love God lavishly. David danced until he became naked before the ark of the Lord. Are you ashamed of God? Take learning from David; he raised an offering to build the house of God that even kings from outside Israel willingly donated. In the opening statement in 1 Chronicles 29, David said - *Now I have prepared with all my might for the house of my God the gold for the things of gold, and the silver for the things of silver, and the brass for the things of brass, the iron for the things of iron, and wood for the things of wood; onyx stones, and stones to be set, stones for inlaid work, and of divers colors, and all manner of precious stones, and marble stones in abundance. Moreover also, because* **"I have set my affection on the house of my God,"** *seeing that I have a treasure of mine own of gold and silver, I give it unto the house of my God, over and above all that I have prepared for the holy house, even three thousand talents of gold, of the gold of Ophir, and seven thousand talents of refined silver, wherewith to overlay the walls of the houses; of gold for the things of gold, and of silver for the things of silver, and for all manner of work to be made by the hands of artificers.* "**Who then offereth willingly to consecrate himself this day unto Jehovah?"**

David explained that the reason he did all this was because he had affection for the things of God. And he opened up a secret, that when we bind our soul unto the altar through our sacrifices, we have become consecrated unto the service of the Lord. Jesus concluded it in Matthew 6:21: *For where your treasure is, there will your heart be also.*

Solomon sacrificed to the amazement of everyone, and even God came down, and later asked Solomon what he needed from the throne of grace. It is what you cherish that you love. It is what you love that you become mindful of. When you become mindful of something, you will want to preserve it. Your desire to preserve it will make you want to spend your time and resources to keep it. In an attempt to keep it, you make it desirable by others so that what you have cherished and loved would become a mark of attraction for you.

This is why a suitor would buy perfumes and gifts for his bride to be. And after marriage, if the man fails to make his wife adorable, there is quarrelling in the home. When you adore your wife and lavish her with gifts, she has no choice but to reciprocate that gesture towards you. You sustain wealth by sustaining relationships. And the ultimate relationship you must keep is God.

The Bible opens our understanding to this in 1 Samuel 2:7-9: *The Lord maketh poor, and maketh rich: he bringeth low, and lifteth up. He raiseth up the poor out of the dust, and lifteth up the beggar from the dunghill, to set them among princes, and to make them inherit the throne of glory: for the pillars of the earth are the Lord 's, and he hath set the world upon them. He will keep the feet of his saints and the wicked shall be silent in darkness.* The Lord does all this to establish whomever He has called to be His saints; hence He is keeping their feet. You can only sustain wealth when you are in the circle of influence of God.

From what we read above, He is keeping the feet of His saints, and as such anyone who would relate with his saints shall in like manner have his or her feet established on earth.

If you want to cross the border of poverty onto the side of wealth, let it be known to you that you would be engaging the powers of the immortal realm continuously to come to your aid, and you can't afford to break the rules that establish wealth in your place. One such rule is the tithe. If however the tithe is from dubious means, there is no need to pay it, because God cannot give a dubious thing. The tithe is ten percent of whatever wealth the Lord has given you power to make. Income from dubious sources cannot be tithe unto the Lord – it should be paid at the altar of the devil. If the tithe is from stealing, God does not steal. We should not use Isaiah 61:6 as a yardstick to steal. God didn't say we should take what is stolen from another in that portion of the Bible.

Another is being on the side of the servant of God always – meaning you must support him to the extent that he can pick your calls in the dead of the night. Many have asked me how they can know a genuine servant of God, and all I tell them is that there is no fake servant of God. One is either a servant of God or a servant of the devil. Do not follow someone who preaches with good oratory skills as a confirmation of one speaking from God if such words don't carry the power of God. If you will not go after your heart's desire, but seek after the mind of God as said in Matthew 6:33, seeking first the Kingdom of God and His righteousness, you will find the servant of God, as you listen to His message of salvation and righteousness, and watch him live the life he preaches. But if your heart is how to make wealth overnight, then you may be dining with the devil. God works with the principle of patience and longsuffering. Don't forget that the job of a servant of God is to preach the gospel and set the captives free.

To make wealth, you are moving into the snare of the devil, and he would hold you captive again, and even throw you into deeper prisons. But if you desire wealth and still want to be free from the devil's net, then your wealth must support the work of God, so that from time to time the Angels of the Lord are sent around you to prevent the devil from holding you hostage. How you treat the servant of God in your midst has a lot to do in this. If you also do not have a personal relationship with God to the extent that you are ready to sponsor crusades, build churches, give scholarships, care for the poor, care for the servants of God, etc., don't seek wealth, because you would be left alone to the manoeuvring of the devil. This is why in the Bible we read of such statements from those who follow the path of the Lord – *if I have found favour*. This statement is reference to obedience to His command and sacrifices made at His altar.

In another instance we see that our declaration of faith in God has a lot to do with our works in His vineyard – James 2:18: *Yea, a man may say, Thou hast faith, and I have works: shew me thy faith without thy works, and I will shew thee my faith by my works.* So, instead of spending all night praying for money to come, get on the side of God, and let your deeds speak on your behalf. There is so much misconception because people often err as a result of doctrinal immaturity regarding deeds. You don't need deeds to merit salvation and eternal life, but you need deeds to get the angels to release your inheritance from the dungeon of the devil. The Lord took the land of Canaan from the control of idols and gave it to the altars raised by Abraham and his descendants. Abraham was a prophet, so he didn't need any servant of God to assist him to get his inheritance. But when the children of Israel were to take the land back, they were not God's servants, so God has to use His arm, Moses, and later Joshua, to get it done. I have come across many believers who struggle to make ends meet because they haven't understood the importance of the servant of the Lord in their lives.

On answering the call of the Lord, I heard a voice one morning, as I recounted earlier – *those who know how to swim do not struggle with the water, if you see yourself struggling, then you are about to fail.* This was very informative, and I knew that if I was to succeed, I must seek the assistance of the immortal realm.

As a mark of appreciation, the children of Israel gave Joshua whatever he requested of them when they were in their inheritance – Joshua 19:49-50: *When they had made an end of dividing the land for inheritance by their coasts, the children of Israel gave an inheritance to Joshua the son of Nun among them: According to the word of the Lord they gave him the city which he asked.* When you have made it, you cannot deny the servant of God your assistance to the burden of the Lord he bears. If you deny him, you have also denied yourself his spiritual prowess and stand-in-the-gap. When I go before the Lord to pray, I make various submissions and will place on the list of consideration; those who have been faithful in various areas – working in the vineyard, tithing, offering, prophetic seeds, welfare service, crusades support, etc.

Those who seek wealth must be sure to keep their souls intact. Jesus gave us a clue to this fact in Matthew 8:36,37: *For what shall it profit a man, if he shall gain the whole world, and lose his own soul? Or what shall a man give in exchange for his soul.* From here, we would see that seeking wealth is not sin as many have always thought, but one must be careful not to trade his or her soul, because the soul is what the devil needs as exchange for the wealth you seek.

In verse 37 of the Bible passage we just read, we can see another clue – something has to be used in exchange for your soul. The devil is interested in taking your soul, your attention and right sense of judgement, and gives you wealth in return. This is the beginning of persecution. It means that continually, your soul is in a battlefield and this shows up at the point where you are about to take the decision that brings wealth. Will you keep your soul intact by not giving bribes or cheating or lying? The Bible admonishes us in Proverbs 21:6-7: *The getting of treasures by a lying tongue is a vanity tossed to and fro of them that seek death. The robbery of the wicked shall destroy them; because they refuse to do judgment.* As you try to pull your soul away from the devil's deceit, the servant of the Lord is there at the altar ensuring that the power of the

Lord paves the way for you with favour – and you would hear such statements from the people in charge of the wealth you seek, *'I don't know why, but you have been recommended to have it from above.'*

The devil obeys only one voice, and that is the voice that cast him down to Earth. This voice speaks on your behalf when you become an asset to the Kingdom of God. Even as the devil requires your soul, which he will receive when you worship him (Matthew 4:9) in exchange for wealth, so also God requires your heart, soul and mind before you will receive all the wealth you seek – Matthew 6:33.

If you expect to benefit from the spiritual gift upon the servant of God, also be willing to allow him have from your material wealth – Romans 15:27: *For if the Gentiles have been made partakers of their spiritual things, their duty is also to minister unto them in carnal things.* In support of the servant of God and his needs, Saint Paul also advised – 1 Corinthians 16:1-2: *Now concerning the collection for the saints, as I have given order to the churches of Galatia, even so do ye. Upon the first day of the week let every one of you lay by him in store, as God hath prospered him.* It is on this basis that servants of God expect ten percent of your income as returns because

Abraham paid it to Melchizedek, meaning that anyone who is appointed by Jesus to champion the Melchizedek course also should be honoured with the tithe. However, the collection of money for the upkeep of the saints does not follow a special pattern; it all depends on what the servant of God deems fit, as we see in the letter of Saint Paul above. Joseph collected twenty percent from the people for Pharaoh (Genesis 47:23-24), and if God bought you with the precious blood of Jesus and He is the one providing your finances, will ten percent be too much of a demand to champion the course of the Lord? I don't think so. I hope this elucidation has helped on this matter.

You don't also compare servants of God, they all have their authorities and jurisdiction – they are lords, if you would want to hear the truth. They can ascend realms of spiritual authorities to bring you answers, and if they have physical needs, it is common wisdom that these become your concerns too. Prosperity comes with obedience – 2 Chronicles 31:5: *And as soon as the commandment came abroad, the children of Israel brought in abundance the firstfruits of corn, wine, and oil, and honey, and of all the increase of the field; and the tithe of all things brought they in abundantly*. The verse starts with the word – *As soon as the commandment came abroad!* You do not consider instructions from the oracle of God – you just obey, if you want prosperity. As soon as the servant releases the command, that is when you obey, and trusting God for a reward, you will certainly have a fill of it. No matter how many times you may obey the instruction without results, there will come a time when you will find a result – 1 Kings 18:43: *And he (Elijah) said to his servant, Go up now, look toward the sea. And he went up, and looked, and said, 'there is nothing.' And he said, 'go again seven times.'* At the seventh time, the servant indeed saw a cloud. Many of us are quick to get discouraged when we don't see results early. Remember, God works with patient people who are willing to endure the slow tick of the clock.

A servant of God who has a divine priestly ordination is more than a pastor. The pastor's job ends at the pulpit, the priest's job starts from the pulpit and ends at the altar. The duty of the angels starts from the altar on earth and ends at the golden altar in heaven. Jesus attends to it from the mercy seat. This is why a servant of God with a priestly ordination can appoint pastors who stand at the pulpit to admonish the people. In most cases, the servant of God with a priestly ordination may have multiple gifts with teaching, and prophecy embedded, and these gifts will make him stand out as one with the oracle of God. Now a servant of God with a divine priestly and prophetic anointing is the one that usually raises an altar.

When the Lord spoke to me in 2008 to tell me that He had raised me as a priest, and I was going to undergo training for six years with Him, He was talking about raising one who would be filled with divine secrets concerning the operations of the altar. And when I wrote my second book, *The Altar In Golgotha*, I understood perfectly that, indeed, I had been anointed into a realm of priesthood. Now at the end of the six-year training, I am now writing more of this truth for your information and obedience.

However, if you don't need money to make ends meet or seek wealth, you can just keep yourself to the terms of the salvation agreement you have entered with Christ. Keep away from the devil, and he will keep away from you. If you still need to make ends meet, and the wealth you seek is being occupied by the devil, you need a higher spiritual power to get him out of the way, and one agent of the host of heaven in your midst who can be of help is the servant of God. Consult him and he shall consult the realm for you; he will stand as surety on your behalf so that you will have your way. His work is to engage the angels that will lift that gate of hell for you to cross over from a life of want to wealth, and he will be held responsible for his actions by the heavenly realm. If in the course of this you lose your soul, he will be chastised for aiding and abetting the loss of a soul into the kingdom of the devil. So when you succeed, and are still strong in the faith, remember him always, and he won't stop thanking God on your behalf. Don't forget that for the sake of Abraham, Lot was rescued.

Many servants of God have disconnected many from their altars, and you may see these people going back to their original ill situations or even worse than they were before they came to seek favour from the altar. Some do this prophetically by lifting a bottle of anointing oil up, praying on it that henceforth anyone who is disloyal is disconnected from the altar, and release it to smash on the floor. The moment this happens, once the oil spills, all that had been will begin to take a reverse turn as the devil begin to wade in now that the power that prevented him this far from taking over your possession is no more. Some may just complain in their prayers, as they make a strong case against you and what the work in their hand has suffered as a result of your disloyalty – the effect on evangelism, welfare, etc - and the Lord will send His Angels to investigate, as happened in the days of Sodom and Gomorrah – Genesis 18:20-21: *And the Lord said, Because the cry of Sodom and Gomorrah is great, and because their sin is very grievous; I will go down now, and see whether they have done altogether according to the cry of it, which is come unto me; and if not, I will know*, and as a righteous judge, a warning may be sent to you which would appear in your dreams, but failure to heed may mean disaster. It was this kind of complaint that made the Lord speak in Malachi 3:7-10: *From the days of your fathers ye have turned aside from mine ordinances, and have not kept them. Return unto me, and I will return unto you, saith Jehovah of hosts. But ye say, Wherein shall we return? Will a man rob God? yet ye rob me. But ye say, Wherein have we robbed thee? In tithes and offerings. Ye are cursed with the curse; for ye rob me, even this whole nation. Bring ye the whole tithe into the store- house, that there may be food in my house, and prove me now herewith, saith Jehovah of hosts, if I will not open you the windows of heaven, and pour you out a blessing, that there shall not be room enough to receive it.*

Tread with caution! I know that you would be wondering if the Altar wasn't the Altar of the Lord? Yes!

It is the Altar of the Lord, raised by a faithful servant, and who pleaded that the Lord should take possession of it with His Angels. So the Altar and all Holy Sites are the abode of Angels. The Angels in that Altar listen to the servant of God and he can also make them err against the will of God, in which case all of them will experience the condemnation of God. The servant of God can send them on errands, even into the devil's camp, to get people and their possessions released.

If you understand how Abraham rescued Lot, you will understand how the servant of God engages the immortal realm to get things done. An instance may be seen in 1 Kings 17:22: *And the Lord heard the voice of Elijah; and the soul of the child came into him again, and he revived.* The servant of the Lord is not one person you should play with because he is empowered spiritually. As long as he is within you don't withhold whatever is due him from him. Be careful about him because your life may be at his mercy – Genesis 20:6-7, if the Lord rebukes him before he does what he wants to do, and he obeys, then you have your life back – Luke 9:54-56: *And when his disciples James and John saw this, they said, Lord, wilt thou that we command fire to come down from heaven, and consume them, even as Elias did? But he turned, and rebuked them, and said, Ye know not what manner of spirit ye are of. For the Son of man is not come to destroy men's lives, but to save them.*

Another instance may be seen in the days of Elijah and Elisha. Elijah called fire to consume the prophets of Baal on one occasion (1 Kings 18:40) and about a hundred in another (2 Kings 1:10,12). Elisha called on the bears to devour forty-two children. Despite the famine in the land, the widow gave Elijah her last morsel of bread before provision came her way. Jesus had no farm where he sowed crops, or was working as a carpenter when His ministry commenced, but those He ministered to, who also buried Him in a tomb no one had lain in before, ministered to His need. The servant of God deserves the best from you. See what you are doing to him as what you would do to a messenger from the Lord.

Jesus says you should bless those who come to you in the name of the Lord – Luke 13:35: *Behold, your house is left unto you desolate: and verily I say unto you, Ye shall not see me, until the time come when ye shall say, Blessed is he that cometh in the name of the Lord.* A confirmation of this is what happened in 2 Chronicles 26:5: *And he sought God in the days of Zechariah, who had understanding in the visions of God: and as long as he sought the Lord, God made him to prosper.* Here, Zechariah was the servant of the Lord, and as long as he was sought after, the king, though he was only sixteen years old, Uzziah succeeded. If Abraham would host angels who were on their way to Sodom, not that they had the intention of seeing him, learn to take care of the servant of God in your midst and you will not lose your reward. End the habit of demanding material things from them. You are the one to provide for them. Jesus didn't have any material possessions to give out to the poor. Even the man He commanded to sell all he had and give to the poor that were about Him needing material things disobeyed Him (Matthew 19:21-22). To tell the extent in which the poor also demanded material help from Him, we would see that when the alabaster oil was poured on Him, the disciples made reference to the poor, because the poor were the burden they were bearing. People have accused Judas of that, but the reason Judas spoke was that he was the one holding the moneybag and he may have been troubled by many poor people – Mark 14:3-9. A confirmation of this would also be the statement of Jesus after He fed them, when they came looking for Him – John 6:26: *Jesus answered them and said, Verily, verily, I say unto you, Ye seek me, not because ye saw the miracles, but because ye did eat of the loaves, and were filled.*

If you want wealth, you must be a giver – Luke 6:38: *Give, and it shall be given unto you; good measure, pressed down, and shaken together, and running over, shall men give into your bosom. For with the same measure that ye mete withal it shall be measured to you again.* We have read how the Lord wrought wonders through His servants to the extent of destroying thirty-one kings (Joshua 12). The truth you are reading here holds some of the guided secrets meant for only a few, who have shown interest in knowing what to do to get wealth and are trusted to be faithful and loyal, but I have decided to put it down in black and white, so that you may know and come to appreciate the hurdles that one must cross in the pursuit of wealth making. I am recounting this in this chapter to show you that there are rules governing the making of wealth.

CHAPTER THREE

MAKING WEALTH THE RIGHT WAY

For everything the Lord has made, there is always the right way to secure control over them and make wealth from them to the glory of God. In the book of Genesis 1:26, God said we should have dominion. To have dominion over something means to subdue it under your control. It is what you have control over that you make wealth out of. God has given us His creation to subdue and command to release their substances for our benefits, and when Jacob did, the Bible said – Deuteronomy 32:13: *He (God) made him ride on the high places of the earth, that he might eat the increase of the fields; and he made him to suck honey out of the rock, and oil out of the flinty rock.* Are you prepared to 'suck honey out of the rock and oil out of the flinty rock'? You must listen to the voice of the Lord to know the right way out.

The disciples were at sea fishing with no result until Jesus came and advised them to cast the net on the right side, and when they did they became rich - John 21:6: *And he said unto them, Cast the net on the right side of the ship, and ye shall find. They cast therefore, and now they were not able to draw it for the multitude of fishes.* The obvious difference between the rich and the poor is that while the poor go after contracts, the rich go after contacts. While the poor seeks money before knowing the person behind the money, the rich know the man behind the money before seeking the money. And this is how you eat the riches of the gentiles and glory in their riches – Isaiah 61:6. To have dominion is to Arise and shine – Isaiah 60:1.

And the question comes again, is making wealth sin? No! It is the love of money that is the root of every evil. Money itself is not evil. It is when we begin to see earthly possessions as our life treasures that we would begin to neglect the salvation of the Lord. Salvation comes with wealth because the earth and all that is in it belong to the Lord, who is salvation himself. Before the Lord cursed the earth as a result of Adam's sins, man didn't need to toil to eat the good of the land, it didn't bring thorns and thistles neither is he to eat the herb of the field to become healed from ailments. Man was not supposed to eat bread with the sweat of his face and he was not supposed to die. But sin brought all these pains we now see upon the face of the earth – Genesis 3:17-19: *And unto Adam he (God) said, Because thou hast hearkened unto the voice of thy wife, and hast eaten of the tree, of which I commanded thee, saying, Thou shalt not eat of it: cursed is the ground for thy sake; in toil shalt thou eat of it all the days of thy life; thorns also and thistles shall it bring forth to thee; and thou shalt eat the herb of the field; in the sweat of thy face shalt thou eat bread, till thou return unto the ground; for out of it wast thou taken: for dust thou art, and unto dust shalt thou return.*

God knows how to give His children better things than our earthly parents – Luke 11:11-13: *If a son shall ask bread of any of you that is a father, will he give him a stone? or if he ask a fish, will he for a fish give him a serpent? Or if he shall ask an egg, will he offer him a scorpion? If ye then, being evil, know how to give good gifts unto your children: how much more shall your heavenly Father give the Holy Spirit to them that ask him.* The Holy Spirit is the most precious to God because this is His personality. If God can release His Holy Spirit for you, is it wealth that He cannot give? All you need is know the rules, abide by them, and you are on your way to smiling. If a good man store riches for his children, what will God do when we submit to Him? Remember that God is the only one who is good – Matthew 19:17: *... there is none good but one, that is, God...* so the Bible was actually referring to one who fears God in Proverbs 13:22: *A good man leaveth an inheritance to his children's children.*

It is when we direct all our attention to making money that we will be out of tune with God. The Bible contains stories of several business opportunities that people ventured into and succeeded, using the proceeds to glorify the Lord. The problem I am having with many acclaimed believers is that they have joined the wicked in oppressing the helpless, all in a bid to make money – this is sin against humanity and God.

Should we make money as believers? Yes! The Bible says that the scriptures will make us wise unto salvation – 2 Timothy 3:15: *And that from a child thou hast known the holy scriptures, which are able to make thee wise unto salvation through faith which is in Christ Jesus.* We cannot be hungry physically and claim to be wise and have been saved. If we are in need while the wicked enjoys the good of the land, what then is our inheritance?

The Bible says in Proverbs 13:22: … *the wealth of the sinner is laid up for the just.* If this promise would manifest in our lives, then we must take Isaiah 1:19, to heart: *If ye be willing and obedient, ye shall eat the good of the land.* If fraudsters can dupe us then we aren't in God's covenant yet. The pain we experience on Earth is as a result of the curse God laid on the land when Adam sinned, and if we claim to have been salvaged by the death of Christ, then our own portion of the land has been sanctified by the blood of the Lamb, and our investment in the land will yield increase – these increases are avenues for making wealth too. Jesus grew as a carpenter, and he would have made money from the sale of chairs, tables, etc. Saint John says in 1 John 3:17: *But whoso hath this world's good, and seeth his brother have need, and shutteth up his bowels of compassion from him, how dwelleth the love of God in him.* From this passage of the Bible, John made reference to some people having riches, and he encouraged giving from our riches to assist our brothers as a demonstration of compassion. Now, taking a closer look explains that those who make wealth, and have compassion towards those in need, showcase the love of God. And if we put this in the right context, it means that the power to make wealth is a demonstration of the love of God towards mankind.

The Holy Spirit wisdom has all the experience one can think of. Jesus didn't have any physical investment, but that didn't make Him one without the wisdom to manage investments. The multiplication of the bread and fishes was an investment that brought people looking for Him the following day. The scripture is also profitable to direct because the Holy Spirit inspired it, and since investment opportunities are mentioned in the scriptures, it shows that God is not against your wealth making overtures provided your soul is intact. Saint Paul excelled in his vocation as a master tent builder. Moses excelled as a shepherd with spiritual sense of reasoning, and that was how he sustained his family before the Lord called him. Money making has a lot to do with having and keeping money-making relationships within the Kingdom of God, else the devil will take you unawares.

The Kingdom of God here on earth boasts of the following experienced people – Isaiah 3:2-3: *The mighty man, and the man of war, the judge, and the prophet, and the prudent, and the ancient, The captain of fifty, and the honourable man, and the counsellor, and the cunning artificer, and the eloquent orator.* All these professionals have the experience to guide you. Do you want to make wealth as an army? You have the righteous there too. Are you a judge and seek wealth? You will also seek a judge who is righteous and wealthy to be your mentor. Are you a prophet and wonder if you can be wealthy? Don't follow evil prophets; there are prophets of God who are wealthy through applying the wisdom of God. Are you an accountant and seek wealth? Don't cheat and tell lies, there are prudent saints who are wealthy. So it applies to those in government, engineers, medical doctors, motivational speakers etc. In every profession the Lord has allowed to flourish on earth, the devil only fakes the original, but we are in tune with the Lord and would serve Him in truth and in spirit with all He has blessed us with.

The Lord commanded that we make disciples of every nation. These disciples are in every area of human endeavour, so that the principle of sanctity may live in the hearts of everyone, and we would live not to breach our resolve to follow Jesus.

And again, there are powers you do not see and can discern their form, who must guide you to your inheritance. This is why it is advisable to also engage who engages them – 2 Kings 6:17. As we leave this chapter, take the following to heart:

- Wealth is our Inheritance from the Lord as a mark of our faithfulness to His course here on earth:

- ✓ The Lord is not expecting the sinner to prosper more than His saints - Proverbs 13:22: *A good man leaveth an inheritance to his children's children; And the wealth of the sinner is laid up for the righteous.*

- ✓ The Lord expects that we spend whatever wealth we have made in soul winning - Matthew 6:19–21: *Lay not up for yourselves treasures upon the earth, where moth and rust consume, and where thieves break through and steal: but lay up for yourselves treasures in heaven, where neither moth nor rust doth consume, and where thieves do not break through nor steal: for where thy treasure is, there will thy heart be also.*

- Wealth is not to be wasted but used for the work of the Lord and it should not lead us into covetousness:

- ✓ We must be wise in spending and should not desire another's wealth - Proverbs 21:17: *He that loveth pleasure shall be a poor man: He that loveth wine and oil shall not be rich.* Luke 12:15: *And he (Jesus) said unto them, Take heed, and keep yourselves from all covetousness: for a man's life consisteth not in the abundance of the things which he possesseth*

- ✓ We must be humble, serving the Lord, and should not oppress others in our midst because we are wealthy - 1 Timothy 6:17-19: *Charge them that are rich in this world, that they be not highminded, nor trust in uncertain riches, but in the living God, who giveth us richly all things to enjoy; That they do good, that they be rich in good works, ready to distribute, willing to communicate; Laying up in store for themselves a good foundation against the time to come, that they may lay hold on eternal life.*

- ✓ We must acknowledge that we are blessed by God and should use our riches to serve Him - Ecclesiastes 5:19: *Every man also to whom God hath given riches and wealth, and hath given him power to eat thereof, and to take his portion, and to rejoice in his labour; this is the gift of God.*

- ■ Wealth demands stewardship unto the Lord from us:

- ✓ We shall be requested to give account some day - Matthew 25:14–30. The parable of the talents shows that wealth making demands total accountability even in the way we spend our finances.

- ✓ We should be content with whatever we have at any material time, rather than wearing ourselves out with greed trying to gain the whole world - 1 Timothy 6:6–10: *But godliness with contentment is great gain. For we brought nothing into this world, and it is certain we can carry nothing out. And having food and raiment let us be therewith content. But they that will be rich fall into temptation and a snare, and into many foolish and hurtful lusts, which drown men in destruction and perdition.*

✓ Everything belongs to God, and if we refuse to make returns in support of His great work in our midst we are seen spiritually as having stolen from the Lord - Haggai 2:8: *The silver is mine, and the gold is mine, saith the Lord of hosts.* God gives peace to those who remember Him and stand to erect a house in His name – Haggai 2:9: ... *in this place will I give peace, saith the Lord of hosts.*

■ We must be generous to those in need if we must sustain our wealth, because their unhealthy complaints at the altar of the Lord can turn the face of God against you:

✓ Giving is the trigger that releases out the bullets of favour from the Lord out of his bowel of mercy to hunt down the treasure you seek - Proverbs 11:25: *The liberal soul shall be made fat: and he that watereth shall be watered also himself.* 2 Corinthians 8:7: *Therefore, as ye abound in every thing, in faith, and utterance, and knowledge, and in all diligence, and in your love to us, see that ye abound in this grace also.* We just read that the people of Corinth abound in everything – not withholding from the demand of the work of God unto the poor and to His saints. This is providence for making wealth at work here.

✓ We shouldn't spurn our neighbours if we want the mercy of the Lord, and we shouldn't oppress the poor if we want happiness - Proverbs 14:21: *He that despiseth his neighbour sinneth: but he that hath mercy on the poor, happy is he.* Isn't God fair enough? Yes of course, to have given us the secrets to enduring peace.

✓ If God has blessed you with much, give as you earn - Luke 12:48: … *For unto whomsoever much is given, of him shall be much required: and to whom men have committed much, of him they will ask the more.*

CHAPTER FOUR

WHY PLAN YOUR MONEY?

We are told in Ecclesiastes 7:12 that *wisdom is a defence, and money is a defence: but the excellency of knowledge is, that wisdom giveth life to them that have it.* So the taking here is that those who have wisdom also have the potential to make money and with the money they have they are regarded, respected and defended by those that look up to them.

How can money give us defence when many who have money today live in fear? It is when such money was not gotten with the wisdom of the Lord. Since money makes wealth, we need to plan our money. In Ecclesiastes 10:19, the Bible says: *Money answereth all things.* For this to happen in line with the promise that *the blessing of the Lord, it maketh rich, and he addeth no sorrow with it* – Proverbs 10:22, it is necessary that believers should have an idea about how to make money, plan it and spend it, to the glory of the Lord so that we won't loss our soul in hell. I refer to this idea as, Effective Financial Planning.

To this end, I would define effective financial planning as: *the process of estimating the resources required to address the basic necessities of life in both short and long term instances, such that the means to employing the required resources are taken note of ahead of time by planning and allocating money as the need arises.* Such a plan must also address who does what and on what time frame. It is a process that helps us to convert our wastes into savings, and then turn the savings into investments.

Jesus opened our understanding into what financial planning is all about when He said: "*Suppose one of you wants to build a tower. Will he not first sit down and estimate the cost to see if he has enough money to complete it? For if he lays the foundation and is not able to finish it, everyone who sees it will ridicule him, saying, 'This fellow began to build and was not able to finish.'* - Luke 14:28-30 NIV. Every task we embark on and we are unable to complete will definitely lead to waste, because of the time and energy we have invested. Looking at Jesus' statement holistically, we would see that if the fellow is unable to complete the tower, he will become desperate, depressed in some cases, seeking for funds or regretting what he has spent, and he will suffer high blood pressure, hiding from those he borrowed money from and those that would mock him daily, etc. This would definitely not be a palatable experience; hence we are in this discussion, since such situations often render people faithless as they undergo the pains caused by poor financial planning, and would with time seek after ungodly means to take shame away from their faces. The Lord didn't create the entire world in a day. The creation accounts in Genesis 1 explain that the events happened one after the other, and one foundation became a foundation for the other creation. This is resource planning in action.

The overall desire to help the work of evangelism will make anyone who is wise desire the blessings of God, because His concern is how we would become springs for the out flow of His blessings to the world. Abraham had this concern of the Lord as an undertaking in his call – Genesis 12:3 … *in thee shall all families of the earth be blessed.*

This is what the Psalmist seems to be saying in Psalms 16:5-6: *Lord, you have assigned me my portion and my cup; you have made my lot secure. The boundary lines have fallen for me in pleasant places; surely I have a delightful inheritance* (NIV). This implies that provided we are in tune with God, He has also provided an inheritance for us in pleasant places. The day you were born, God had an inheritance for you and kept angels in its charge, to protect it for you. We also know that the angels of God are holy, meaning that for us to enjoy these inheritances we need to move back into the realm of God. The prodigal son met his father to get his blessing. Many of us have prayed to God to give us our inheritance; that God should grant us our heart desire. God has also released them – we can either be wasteful or cautious. If you don't have the wisdom to plan, you will always beg from others.

Are you going to squander your blessings? God has been protecting your blessings with his angels until you demand them from Him. The prodigal son returned and was welcomed home, but we were not told if he ever got another inheritance, because he had taken all that was entitled to him, which he also squandered. This we can infer from the father's statement to his elder son – Luke

15:31-32: *And he said unto him, Son, thou art ever with me, and all that I have is thine. It was meet that we should make merry, and be glad: for this thy brother was dead, and is alive again; and was lost, and is found.* So the prodigal son will still be poor, living at the mercy of his elder brother because he has squandered his own inheritance with harlots.

The blessings are falling in pleasant places – God cannot hate you to have kept your blessings far away from you. His word says that He will raise prophets among you. If you have to travel hundreds of kilometres to get your anointing, then you may be missing it already. Since the Lord makes your blessings fall in pleasant places, you need also to invest in pleasant places. Wasting your blessings on harlots is not a pleasant investment, because harlotry is not a pleasant job. King David testified that his cup runs over in Psalms 23:5; as your own cup starts to run over, get a bowl and keep the cup inside so that the increase will become gathered and invested. This is wisdom. In your prayers, tell God to keep your blessings in pleasant places.

God will not keep your blessings in the sea for you to labour to get them, or in the wilderness, or among thorns, but they will fall in pleasant places in the name of Jesus

– Amen! You should not despise those God has raised for you, who would take you to your inheritance thinking you can run to those who are popular to anoint you – you may never get it. It has to be Moses, then Joshua who Moses handed over to. There is someone the Lord has given the task to who will lead you into your inheritance. This usually becomes words of wisdom and advice you will hear daily as you grow hearing the word of God and reading related books, like the one you are holding now, written by anointed servants of God.

Some have asked me why they cannot hear from God directly. You hear from a realm you subscribe to. Each of these realms has training grounds in the form of cloudy tabernacles administered by servants of God. If you are faithful to the ministry of a servant of God, you will hear from his realm. I remember some fellows who were close to me then and they were hearing from the realm and seeing too, who then felt God was using them and they became arrogant. When they left, they discovered that they couldn't hear nor see again. They would have to struggle through days and nights of prayers, and what God would do was to lead them to one of his servants again. They only had that gift to assist me, but they misused it and then lost it.

In most cases God will speak to you through his voice, just as Samuel heard the voice of Eli and ran down to him three times, until Eli sensed that God was the one speaking to Samuel. This is the reason you see some pastors submitting under other servants of God. You need an Eli, the servant of God, who will teach you how to hear God speak. The book of Proverbs 1:6 says that there are *dark sayings*. These dark sayings are only released to those who seek to look further into the dark.

But one thing is sure; lack of planning will make us lose all that God had given to us, unless we meet Him to teach us the wisdom that will help us secure our future today, by planning financially. And this would be seen in Psalms 119:35-37: *Direct me in the path of your commands, for there I find delight. Turn my heart toward your statutes and not toward selfish gain. Turn my eyes away from worthless things;* (NIV)

Effective financial planning is possible when God:

- Directs us in the path of His commands and turns our heart toward His statutes so that we can live in righteousness because: *He makes poor, and makes rich. He brings low, He also lifts up* – 1 Samuel 2:7.

- Helps to turn our heart away from things that will bring us selfish gain.
- Turns our eyes from worthless things.

From these we would see that to effectively plan our finances, we need:

- Direction - advice
- Not to be selfless in our desires – think about others too.
- Invest for posterity – believe that tomorrow never comes, get it done today.

If we look at these, we see that the reason people are unable to plan financially, and then live a life that will make them not love money, is captured as what the eyes see – Psalms 119:37: *Turn away mine eyes from beholding vanity.* Many of us desire anything our eyes see. Whether they are worth desiring or not, we spend our sweat on worthless things that have no long-lasting value. Worthless spending is like counting the stars in the night sky with the hope that one day he or she would know the total number of the stars that fill the sky. This spending would include buying extravagant items - cars, houses, clothes, perfume, etc. Anything we purchase which will empty our pockets to the extent that we become slaves to the pursuit of money is not worth dying for.

But if we see God as the ultimate reason why we are living, we can avoid waste, and the love of it. The Bible says of Job's reasoning as he experienced denials due to the affliction of the devil: *If I have put my trust in gold or said to pure gold, 'You are my security,' if I have rejoiced over my great wealth, the fortune my hands had gained,* ***then these also would be sins to be judged, for I would have been unfaithful to God on high*** – Job 31:24, 25, 28 NIV. The highlighted texts prove the point that we sin when we worship our materials of wealth.

Many of us see the possessions of our hand - gold and great wealth - as our security, and God's concern is that because of lack of the ability to plan financially, which now makes us waste our finances on these items, we are becoming poor and chasing after money to the extent that many of us have neglected Him, and our days of rest have been prolonged because our hearts follows wherever our needs lie (Matthew 6:19-21). But one thing we must know is this; that our days are in the hands of the Lord and therefore whatsoever we have today we should ensure they are not accumulations of waste that would perish someday. Every man stands as long as he breathes, hence our lives are but *handbreadths* – Psalms 39:5. So we would say that our end is like a breath away. Why should we then waste every 'breath' of our lives in worthless desires?

Another verse of the Bible that buttresses what we just discussed above and will help us to understand better what financial planning is all about is Proverbs 21:17: *He who loves pleasure will become poor; whoever loves wine and oil will never be rich.* And from this verse we can see why poverty becomes:

- The love for pleasure
- The love for wine – merriment
- The love of oil – luxury

And all these will lead to the love of money, as such a person will want to make money by all means possible to refill his or her drained pocket.

One other reason why people become poor is that they see themselves as having attained the height of success in life and would not want to seek the kind of wisdom that will enable them to increase in finance. This is also why we learnt from the Bible in Proverbs 13:7 that:

One man pretends to be rich, yet has nothing; another pretends to be poor, yet has great wealth. And this would imply that the reason why some get richer by the day is because they always see themselves as poor and act a life of simplicity and humility, while those who are often proud, pretending to be rich when they are not, would always be poor due to pride – Proverbs 29:23: *A man's pride shall bring him low: but honour shall uphold the humble in spirit.* Anyone who is proud is not a good financial planner, as they would find it difficult to learn from their financial spending mistakes.

The discussion so far proves that from our homes to society, one thing is common, and this is waste. Take a look around your surroundings and count the examples of waste. Name them one by one and it will surprise you what a mess we have caused in our lives. While people may see excreta as essential waste, it could be argued that the quantity of human faeces at every given time could actually explain how we waste money on foods. Visiting restaurants would also prove to you that we waste so much food that shouldn't have been cooked or even bought. On the issues on food wastage, God gave manna and expected that each family would take the amount they could eat, and Jesus also ensured that the remaining baskets of bread were gathered. Even while we see our excreting products as essential wastes, non-essential wastes include items of beauty, unused clothes that we would eventually not be using for years to come which fill our wardrobes, cars that we would not drive in months – deteriorating in value daily, etc.

We all need to learn from our financial mistakes as we read this book. It is a mystery how many of us have helped others to succeed in life through the financial advices we have given to them while we still remain where we had been before they met us for a simple opinion which obviously they have digested, and now they are shining stars.

Instead of being the advisor always, we should try to put into practice the wisdom we have inside of us, so that others may watch what we do, learn from it, and become shining stars like us. It is time to look inward and think "me!" This will enable us take this discussion seriously to heart, so that we can see the reason to make amends in our financcs. Thc importance of financial planning cannot be over emphasized, due to the obvious influence it has on our homes, society, government, and even in the church. Every organisation that has gone bankrupt has done so due to mismanaged funds occasioned by lack of effective financial planning.

CHAPTER FIVE

FINANCIAL PLANNING THOUGHTS

This is what the Lord says … *"Break up your unplowed ground and do not sow among thorns"* - Jeremiah. 4:3. Implying further that we need to invest wisely, relate with people efficiently and live in an environment that does not grow thorns – hatred, gossip, jealousy, etc. This is the power of wealth making and financial planning.

Breaking fallow ground and avoiding sowing among thorns will only come when we are diligently engrossed with decisions that will add value to our lives, and then instead of living a life of waste, we may employ the wisdom of God in helping us to plan financially, and then spend and invest wisely.

The devil has taken the hearts of many away from God

and possessed them with the spirit of mammon so that they will ever chase after money. People visit all manner of spiritualists and prophets in search for money, and to receive wisdom on how to live a successful life. The wisdom packed into this book will take you out of pain as the Lord opens your eyes to how you can effectively plan your finances and have enough time to serve God gloriously. This section of this book is inspired through the wisdom in the books of Ecclesiastes 10:10, Jeremiah 4:3, Matthew 25:14-30 and Exodus 3:7-8. We will be looking into these verses of the Bible to have a fair understanding of what I feel are the school of thoughts that centres on financial planning:

1. **Wisdom is the root of financial planning:** This can be inferred from Ecclesiastes 10:10: *If the iron is blunt, and one does not sharpen the edge, he must use more strength, but wisdom helps one to succeed* – (ESV). The financial planner is always engrossed with finding an easier, cost effective and productive way of getting things done. In life, I have seen that there is always a better and cheaper way to get things done. If you will fill your heart with this wisdom of getting things done better and yet cheaper, you are already on your way to becoming a wise money spender. So what we are

learning from this verse is: instead of wasting your energy trying to achieve your set goals through trial and error, you could apply wisdom, knowing what to jettison and what to accept, as a burden that you would bear, so that even in the presence of storms, you are still better off, without getting drowned in the sea of the worries of survival. I encourage you to pay the price to acquire wisdom, it is worth the price – buy books and read. Many people don't value what they haven't spent a dime on. Honour those through whom you get wisdom – Pharaoh honoured Joseph and Nebuchadnezzar honoured Daniel. Those who spend to get wisdom are those with a sense of direction – Proverbs 17:16: *Why should a fool have money in his hand to buy wisdom when he has no sense.* Calamities befall those who don't have wisdom (Proverbs 1:26). Since it is difficult to predict when calamities will befall a man, *as it comes like a whirlwind* - Proverbs 1:27, it is advisable that one seek all available wisdom as it is always there waiting for you to seek - *Wisdom cries aloud in the street, in the markets she raises her voice; at the head of the noisy streets she cries out; at the entrance of the city gates she speaks* (Proverbs 1:1). The reason why the fool fail in life is not because someone hates them, it is because they hate wisdom, as the

Bible tells us – Proverbs 1:32: *For the simple are killed by their turning away, and the complacency of fools destroys them.* Complacency is the act of self-righteousness. This is what destroys many believers too – 'I don't need to submit under any servant of God, I can talk to God myself.' This same habit is what they take wherever they go, and would not want to seek knowledge from anybody. Those who turn away from advice end up early in the grave.

2. **There is need for new investments:** We can only invest wisely when we are ready to break new ground and where there is less competition. This is the singular reason why pioneers of various manufactured products often do well, and stay long in business. In Jeremiah 4:3, which we have been digesting, we are faced with this fact of hard investment – breaking up fallow ground. In agricultural terms, fallow ground holds more manure due to the presence of decaying and decomposing substances – plants and animals. Sowing on 'fallow grounds' is capital intensive because such activity involves money to cut down big trees, tilling the soil, and coping with wild animals, etc. These are the uncertainties that we must note as we venture out. Capital-intensive projects save your

money for the future, when they will also appreciate overtime.

3. **Don't sow among thorns:** I decided to use the statement the way it is stated in Jeremiah 4:3. What is sowing among thorns? – It could infer that we may be investing in:
   - The wrong business
   - Having bad advisers
   - Revealing our secrets to enemies who are disguised as friends
   - Having a spouse who wastes
   - Living in a house which our income can't maintain
   - Unwise expenses on perishable items
   - Wasting money on unwanted cars
   - Spending money to impress people or belong to an exorbitant class to earn pride, etc.

All these avenues will definitely bring our downfall. Invest every second, every minute, every hour, every day, month and year! If you think of being a blessing to somebody, then you won't want to live a life of want. Don't eat all your increase. What you desire is what comes to you. The blessings of the Lord are likened unto children; if you hate children they will run away from you.

The kind of church you attend will also affect you. It could be a thorn. If you attend a church where you have to be fighting witches and wizards, you may find it hard to move forward. Those who sit on a can of gunpowder will always have their sorrows right before them. The power of God in you is more than the power of all the witches put together. The Bible says that we are wrestling with principalities in power manifesting as the wisdom of the world. One of such is the TV, and another is social networking. Your phone can be, even the Internet can be a shadow of principalities.

4. **Become a trusted and productive financial custodian:** This is one lesson that will quickly pop into your mind as you go through the parable of the talents in Matthew 25:14-30: Jesus' emphasis here was how one would become a trustworthy and productive finance planner and manager. The best way to know if you will not come to poverty is when you can account for every money you spend, and learn from your spending mistakes. A time came when I had to record my financial spending habits for over a period, and after I plotted the graph of the difference between

my income and expenses, I discovered that the graph was always on the negative or on the 'zero' line. This was how I sat down to study the word of God and started putting it to practice. This is how to be a trusted and productive financial custodian. Such a person always seeks avenues through which he or she can increase sources of financial opportunities so as to grow his or her savings and investments. This is what will make a person take both the physical and spiritual laws governing financial increase seriously. Spiritually speaking, such a person would not want to eat his or her tithes, failing in paying of vows, supporting the work of God in various other capacities, etc. Physically speaking, such a person will treat customers nicely, knowing that his or her financial success depends on them. They will want to open up their heart to learning new and better ways of investment. They will be very mindful of the attitude they display in order not to scare away people that would help them succeed financially. As advised by Jesus, the most important commandment of a trusted and productive financial planner is love, which shows in the way he or she goes about his or her daily financial activities.

5. **Thinking increase:** What we think is who we become over time. The lord say there is a better land flowing with milk and honey (Exodus 3:7-8). This is all a good financial planner sees. And because the heart is fixed on achieving increase in all you do, there is no way you will waste tomorrow's proceeds today.

How can we do all this if we don't have the right financial planning experience? We can see that effective financial planning has the power to help us determine short and long-term financial goals and create a balanced plan to meet these goals. So financial planning is more about:

- Goal setting
- Budgeting.
- Fund-seeking through the employment of adequate resources.
- Spending on what is needful at the material time, based on ranked importance of available priorities.
- Reserving enough for a rainy day.
- Monitoring of expenses and investments.

CHAPTER SIX

EFFECT OF LACK OF FINANCIAL PLANNING

While trying to get a basis for measuring where we can avoid waste, I stumbled on consumer spending habit figures released in the United States. The 2013 figures of annual spending released by the Bureau of Labor Statistics, US Department of Labor[1], showed that spending for the year by consumers was high in three major areas in the following descending order – housing, transportation and food. This would be typical of what happens around the world. Is it possible to spend less on housing by living in cheaper apartments? Can we reduce the number of cars we have so that we can spend less on fuel? Can we stop buying new cars and make do with our old cars, provided they can still serve the purpose of mobility? Is it not possible to walk rather than spend money on transportation? Can't we minimise our air travel? Must we always take vacations by air? What about food – is it not possible that we can spend less? We must answer these questions before we can read further. This is where we will start getting value from our waste.

From the same source, a further average spending breakdown for 2013 of some selected components showed the trend in the following descending order: vehicle purchases ($3,271) – gasoline ($2,418) – health insurance ($2,418) – apparel ($1,604) – cash contributions to churches and religious organisations ($699). Where did all the money go? Cars, fuels, health insurance, fashion, and the least to God's kingdom and humanitarian services. The closer we are to our sources of income, the less we spend on cars and the less fuel. The more we stop eating junk food, the less we become afraid of health-related expenses. The more we give to God's work, the more He will take away sorrow from us.

Now that we have explained the school of thought that centres around effective financial planning from the preceding chapters, let's quickly take a look at some outcomes of lack of effective financial planning. To do this, we are going to list some of the things that armed robbers, soldiers at war, public enterprise and government leaders, some servants of God, men, women, young people and children usually fall in love with:

- **Armed robbers:** Those who carry out the act of robbery usually focus their attention on the stealing of money, jewelleries, raping of women, cars, electronic goods, guns, etc. All robbers take hard drugs and alcoholic drinks.
- **Secular musicians:** These people spend their money on cars, women for sex, clubbing, etc.
- **Soldiers of war:** In the Bible we see that the reason Saul was rejected by God was for the spoil he carted away after defeating the Amalekites – 1 Samuel 15:9: *But Saul and the people spared Agag, and the best of the sheep, and of the oxen, and of the fatlings, and the lambs, and all that was good, and would not utterly destroy them: but every thing that was vile and refuse, that they destroyed utterly.* Many soldiers all over the world, and even in the days of the Bible, in most cases take money, women for sex, children to become their servants, jewellery, electronic goods, guns, swords, horses, heads of leaders or taking them alive, etc., along with them after being victorious. One would also see many of them taking alcoholic drinks and hard drugs.

- **Public enterprise and government leaders:** Both in the public and government sector there are reports of how these leaders have stolen money. Many also have concubines who they waste money on. Others indulge in night clubbing activities and would take all manner of hard drugs in some cases and also drink alcohol.
- **Some servants of God:** It has also been heard recently of servants of God wasting money on things of the world – unnecessary travelling overseas and the buying of jets, and some other unworthy investments.
- **Men:** They want to be noticed and respected. This is the element of the hurting ego in them and they want to have the best cars, women for sex, stay in the best hotels and live in expensive houses as they try to display their show of superiority over their peers, expensive designer items – wrist watches, shirts, belts, shoes, etc. As they live this life, they also become wasters, and these desires tend to drive them crazy over the chasing of more money to make ends meet. As they do that, their attention for God diminishes.
- **Women:** Women want more money, more jewellery, more designer shoes, clothes, perfumes, and handbags, deodorants, eating junk foods, etc.

- **Young people:** They spend their earnings on illicit sex, drinking, clubbing and expensive cars, and want to be seen as keeping up with fashion.

- **Children:** Children eat all manner of food. They love toys to play with and want to go to places for sightseeing. They don't save but want the money given to them to be used now. When adults begin to eat food meant for children such as chocolates, meat, eggs, etc., then you are opening up your life to sickness that will waste your money.

The love of the items of pleasures listed above is all an avenue for waste and is the reason behind people chasing after money. So it is easy to know when one is going to become poor. The only avenue to avoid poverty, chase of money, denying God His time, etc., is through financial planning.

Now why do these people go after all this without a sense of decorum? The Bible will tell us why:

- Jesus' temptation came at a time when He had become hungry – Matthew 4:2-3: *And when he had fasted forty days and forty nights, he was afterward an hungred. And when the tempter came to him.*

- The angels left heaven to marry the daughters of men, because they wanted to have a taste of freedom to choose whatever they want and not what pleases God – Genesis 6:2: ... *the sons of God saw that the daughters of man were attractive. And they took as their wives any they chose.* When we cannot show restraint in what we desire we will definitely not be wise in financial planning.

- Adonijah begged the mother of Solomon to give him the virgin that was sent to become David's wife, had he survived the illness that led to his death (1 Kings 2). The desperate desire by many men to have a wife has also ruined their lives, as is seen in rival cult groups in institutions of learning.
- Solomon's idolatrous wives lured him into idolatry. When people yield their hearts to the worship of idols, there is no way they will plan. Solomon was a successful wealthy king, but no trace of his wealthy empire survived till this day, because God took the kingdom from him as a result of his sinful atrocities.
- The gold and silver in the temple in Jerusalem were carted away by the Babylonian king Nebuchadnezzar.
- The children of Israel used the gold they took from Egypt with them to make a golden calf, an idol they later worshipped and paid obeisance to.

Haven't we seen all the things that waste our money and make it hard for us to plan for posterity with the money the Lord had entrusted in our hands? All this points to the fact that the devil is behind all these acts, because he engages the heart of men to love these things so that they will live a life of waste. But Jesus says He has overcome the world, meaning that anyone who is in Christ is not supposed to experience the life of waste that will make him or her chase after money. This implies that the lack of financial planning is caused by our indulgence in habits of pleasure and personal gratification.

Effective financial planning is the solution to all we have been discussing. It will help you to be conscious of the following:

- Trusting in God always: Proverbs 18:10-11
- Righteous standing before God: Proverbs 11:4
- Apply wisdom in your drive for wealth. You must not have everything: Proverbs 23:4-5
- Do the best today, don't expect too much from tomorrow. What you achieve today is what tells to what extent tomorrow will yield its fruits. Leave no stone unturned today. You must make maximum use of today, as if it is all you've got. Make it a duty to account for every second God has given you – it is the finite

element of financial planning. Tomorrow may never come - Proverbs 27:1: *Do not boast about tomorrow, for you do not know what a day may bring* (ESV).

- Don't restrain your hands – stretch them out to bless others and engage your hands also in doing something that will bring reward to you and others - Ecclesiastes 4:5: *The fool folds his hands and eats his own flesh* (ESV).
- Engage other people in working – a man must involve his wife and then the children in what he does, because the reward will be better when more hands are involved - Ecclesiastes 4:9-10: *Two are better than one, because they have a good reward for their toil. For if they fall, one will lift up his fellow. But woe to him who is alone when he falls and has not another to lift him up.*

■ Do not seek for wealth because you are envious of somebody, even though you plan financially. Such plans will be devoid of the wisdom of God, and you will end up with a hasty financial plan that will cause you more pain - Ecclesiastes 4:4: *Then I saw that all toil and all skill in work come from a man's envy of his neighbour. This also is vanity and a striving after wind* (ESV).

- In your planning, make time for leisure, as all work and no play makes Jack a dull boy.

All we have said above will stand out as items that we must treat when we practise financial planning. We will know what we need, where to get it, how to get it and what we must do to retain it.

All we have seen, as the reason for hasty wealth and lack of effective money planning, is caused by the spirit of mammon, aimed at taking the minds of the children of God far away from Him. I curse every spirit of mammon moving around you to make you lose your inheritance and waste financially in the name of Jesus – Amen. The Lord says that your blessings are falling in pleasant places. The anointing of the Lord is upon you – whatever your hand finds to do shall increase. Ever since creation, the rains have never stopped falling. As you go out your blessings will fall in pleasant places. You will not search far. The sea doesn't produce any water, yet it receives water from all sources. So shall your increase be in the name of Jesus – Amen.

CHAPTER SEVEN

THE SPIRIT OF FINANCIAL PLANNING

The desire to succeed is what would make you want to plan your money. The Bible says - Proverbs 22:3: *A prudent man sees danger and takes refuge, but the simple keep going and suffer for it* (NIV). When you look at nations that are suffering from economic austerity today, you will notice great laxity – their citizens hardly work because the state pays even the unemployed, and feeds prisoners so well that many would prefer to lock up their intelligence and waste in prison houses – Isaiah 42:22. In most cases they have also abandoned the Lord and are therefore visited with plagues – Zechariah 14:18: ... *there shall be the plague wherewith Jehovah will smite the nations that go not up to keep the feast of tabernacles.* It is only when we hand over our treasures unto the Lord, and He possesses it as holy unto Himself, that we will have enough to always eat from His holy pots – Zechariah 14:20-21.

The spirit of financial planning brings far-sightedness. A prudent man thinks ahead, and then plans his finances to take care of unforeseen contingencies. This was the advice Joseph gave to Pharaoh, else death would have visited many nations if Egypt wasn't there surviving on Joseph's advice. A financial planner watches and then understands the vision ahead of him - Daniel 8:15: *While I, Daniel, was watching the vision and trying to understand it...*(NIV). Your breakthrough may be just before you in the form of a veiled spiritual handwriting on the wall – you need it decoded. Your level of understanding, physically and spiritually, will help you out of want. The reason many are living a life of emptiness and deprivation is deeply rooted in their inability to understand spiritual codes. The Bible espouses this also in Isaiah 6:9: ... *Hear ye indeed, but understand not; and see ye indeed, but perceive not.* And for this reason those who don't have spiritual understanding would be afflicted with confusion – Isaiah 6:10: *Make the heart of this people fat, and make their ears heavy, and shut their eyes; lest they see with their eyes, and hear with their ears, and understand with their heart, and convert, and be healed.*

If I tell you to pick up a plain A4 piece of paper for instance and look into it with all your mental focus, and that you will eventually see something written on it. You will probably want to give it a trial, knowing that I am a prophet, and after some deep insightful look into it, you will discover that there is nothing written on it, the paper is still a plain sheet of paper. But if on second thoughts you decide to write down your wish on the paper, you will discover that you have more words written down than you had ever imagined in life. This is where financial planning starts. From the items you have written down, you are going to classify them into two major headings – immediate needs and future needs. If you, however, decide to go for the future needs now, you are wasting resources already, because the future needs are only your wants.

So, we are imbibing the spirit of financial planning already as we go for items that will add value to our lives, reduce financial stress on us and reduce pressure on available income and resources. The resources we waste include gas for our cookers and electricity – switching on bulbs that are not needed and too much use of electronic goods such as TVs. Sometimes we over-stress our resources, including ourselves, trying to make more money, and then they become worn out as a result, causing us to have sleepless nights as we try to get more money to acquire new equipment.

Since we know that finance is needed in the home, church, society and the industry, we must imbibe the spirit of financial accountability. We will discuss this principle of financial planning below.

Effective financial planning helps in the following ways:

- **Planning for old age:** Many will discover after so many years of working that they haven't being planning for the days of their old age. And so in old age they will become the burden of the local church, their rich relatives, children, NGOs or the government, as they often see these people and establishments as philanthropists who should provide for their up keeping. Many would have not been able to raise up worthy children as many were raised outside God-fearing homes, and these children who have become wayward would even add to their grief at old age. Many honestly don't think about old age while they are still being carried away by the frenzies celebrations of youth. Even as a righteous man, there is still evidence in the Bible that we may be ill before death. Many may say it is not their portion: Isaac had poor vision in old age, Elisha was sick unto death, Peter was blind. When Jesus told Peter what would befall him in old age, it made him start thinking what amount of salary he would pay to the 'help' that would eventually lead him around when he finally walked blind. In old age, as in most cases, many of us may have lost our spouses, and if the children are also no more - maybe they died earlier due to accidents - then what will your old age be like? These are all practical questions begging for your financial planning answers. Enrolling in a pension scheme is good and you should consider one. You can meet with your bank manager for a discussion on planning for old age – they are of great help.

- **Children's school fees:** Many only start trying to pay their children's school fees when the school resumes, so most children are driven out of school because the school fees were not paid when due. Many also, without minding their salaries, have placed their children in schools with high fees. I do not believe that high school fees will finally improve a child's intelligence and good manners. It is the extra work done by the parents to lead the child in the ways of the Lord that turns a child into a successful adult.

- **Pay tax:** If we don't pay our taxes, there would be no roads and other social amenities. Jesus paid tax. The disciples caught a fish, and in its mouth was a coin He used to pay for tax – Matthew 17:27: *Notwithstanding, lest we should offend them, go thou to the sea, and cast an hook, and take up the fish that first cometh up; and when thou hast opened his mouth, thou shalt find a piece of money: that take, and give unto them for me and thee.* If you evade taxes, you will be arrested. This is why your investment must yield increase so that you get tax from it, just as the fish brought out the tax payment from its mouth. Can you find a spiritual link to wealth from the miracle of the coin in the fish's mouth?
- **Medical bills:** It is a good thing to have something saved for medical bills. There is also medical insurance cover that one can contribute towards. You can ask your doctor for advice. We work every day, and do not practise the kind of rest that would enable the tissues in our body to recycle themselves. Many of us live in dirty environments that are infested with diseases. As long as we live in messy environments, we should be ready to face the diseases that breed there. Good health comes with wisdom. If you eat junk foods, be ready to have some money saved to cure

illnesses. The cry for healing miracles has rendered many believers "hopeless" as they run from one prayer meeting to the other. And this has watered down their perception of who Christ is – to them He is a miracle-working God, and not one filled with the power and wisdom to enable them live a worthy life, giving them the knowhow to run the government, manage businesses, manage their marriages, train their children, etc. The mindset of a miracle-working God is what is affecting many, and they have lost grip on the real benefit of salvation - that is, having life and having it more abundantly – John 10:10.

- **Having a philanthropist's heart**: The Bible says "there is one that scattereth" – to give requires that you should set aside some amount for that. The Bible portion referred to above actually says: *There is one that scattereth and yet prospereth* –Proverbs 14:24. A philanthropist does not become poor because he is giving – Proverbs 28:27: *He that giveth unto the poor shall not lack: but he that hideth his eyes shall have many a curse.* Though this would also mean large-scale investment where one has to employ the poor for a pay that would help them meet their responsibilities. Some see this passage as meaning that one has to waste money in parties where they provide food enough for people to eat and then go back home regretting what they had spent. You also don't give out what you have borrowed – that would make you a debtor and make you poorer. If you must borrow, then it must be invested in such a way that the investment will pay the interest on the loan, and then pay you for your labour and managerial efforts.

- **Learning:** We can also set aside funds for training ourselves in other areas and works of life so that you can be relevant every day you are called to offer service. As you do this you will become well informed of recent happenings in job circles. Also try to pay for information, even if it is from your spouse – not just a thank you, but let it go with some money. It is not good to take the knowledge in people for free. This is why we give offerings or pay for seminars. Do not photocopy books to read, unless there is a 'no copyright' notice. Books are proprietary materials. It is a criminal offence to infringe on the rights of the copyright owner. A woman was very ill, including the members of her family, and she met me for prayers after armed robbers had robbed her on her way from the office. While I was ministering to her I got a revelation that she had photocopied a book on healing written by a servant of God. She accepted this when I asked her, and I told her to go and ask for forgiveness. She did so, and later she bought some copies of the book and gave them out free and she and her family were restored. Spend money to buy books, music, videos, and other media-related items of knowledge. This way you will begin to accept the fact that nothing is free. This habit will also help you to start giving a worthy offering to God. A good financial planner does not always think of what to gain from others, but what to offer. His or her philosophy is *give more unto others, what you want them give to you.*

- **Leisure:** Someone who plans financially will usually spend time with their family on outings – visiting places for fun. But this should be done cautiously – it shouldn't become too frequent. A couple that plan financially will live to love one another. Isaac sowed from what he had, meaning that he only wanted to go to Egypt so that the family would not run out of food, until God spoke to him. And after that, you would see him and his wife enjoying love – Genesis 26:8: … *behold, Isaac was sporting with Rebekah his wife.*
- **We can assist others to succeed:** Instead of being in a hurry to start our own investment, we can lend our hearts to serve where we are employed. This can only be when we are planning financially, else we will

waste our resources on wasteful items and that will begin to breed dissatisfaction in our hearts, leading us to set up our own investment in a hurry. Becoming a more focused employee where you can climb the ladder of leadership authority through promotion is a good thing to desire. Many people who lack patience wherever they work and often complain of poor income do so due to poor financial planning habits. We have a word of advice in 1 Corinthians 3:6, that Paul planted, and Apollo watered and the Lord gave the increase. Watering is growing for the future. Joshua did not drive his own vision – he continued where Moses stopped, meaning he had been with Moses all the while, learning through Moses how to seek the face of God as Moses did. Elisha was with Elijah throughout Elijah's life, and you wouldn't see Elisha coming to the forefront to get himself announced - he waited his turn. In short, his humility was attested to in 2 Kings 3:11: *And one of the king of Israel's servants answered and said, Here is Elisha the son of Shaphat, which poured water on the hands of Elijah.* The quest for money is the reason for all the level of fake unqualified contractors we have around today, all promising what they cannot deliver. Without learning, there is no transfer of knowledge – this is a fact.

- **Enables one to build for God:** The book of Haggai 1:5 says: *Now therefore thus saith the Lord of hosts; Consider your ways.* Many who complain of money when it is time to build for God do so because they had invested the money wrongly without following financial planning rules. The Bible says we should not sow among thorns (Jeremiah 4:3). Every believer should ask himself or herself if the investment is worth it before venturing into it – this is the beauty of investment planning. Tithing and offerings are spiritual seeds of investment, if sown in the right fallow ground, and not among thorns. Today, we have so many synagogues of Satan, and any tithes paid there weren't paid to God. If God is not in a place, there is no need to pay tithes and offerings there. We give tithes and offerings as a mark of honour to God who gave us the increase, and so, if the increase is not from God why pay the tithe and offering from such an investment which has been founded on the devil's ill wealth? If an armed robber or prostitute, someone who does business by cheating, politician who steals money, etc pays tithes and offerings from such ungodly money, they are making a mockery of God. The Bible says in proverbs 29:24,27: *Whoso is partner with a thief hateth his own soul ... An unjust man is an abomination to* *the just...* Such is the fate of all servants of God accepting tithes and offerings from thieves, prostitutes, politicians who loot the treasury, dubious employees, etc – their souls will perish in hell. God doesn't support any of the ills above, so how can He be pleased with such monies? As believers it is advisable also to set aside money for offering for your Pastor - 1 Corinthians 16:1–2: *Now concerning the collection for the saints, as I have given order to the churches of Galatia, even so do ye. Upon the first day of the week let every one of you lay by him in store, as God hath prospered him, that there be no gatherings when I come.* For me, until I am satisfied that the work of God is not lying fallow, I don't think about myself. On a monthly basis I take out money for evangelism – printing flyers, billboards, book writing, music production, etc., with a bid to announce the gospel of Christ. It makes sense to store in heaven, because whatever is secured spiritually is secured physically. By and large, the Lord has protected my investments with His love and spirit.

- **Accountability:** This is a must as we plan; to account for all that we spend. I did this on my salary after two years and the result wasn't satisfactory. Instead of blaming myself, I learned and made amends, and since then my life hasn't been the same. I have grown from one level of grace and provision to the other, to the amazement of my colleagues.

This is the spirit of effective financial planning. Anything you do in life requires financial planning, even if you are about to gain admission into an institution of learning. King David said God anointed him and his cup ran over. As an anointed child of God, this is what happens to you. To ensure that the blessings running over are not wasted, we need to plan them. Many students have told me they couldn't go to school because they had no sponsor. If they had good financial planning skills they would know whether to get a job and attend a part-time evening programme or work weekends to succeed in school. Most of the students I have encountered are too arrogant to be assisted by anyone who has the heart to help them. They wear the most expensive clothes, and use expensive mobile phones that many who are working wouldn't use.

If you are a young man about to marry and if the lady is wasteful, keep clear unless you see that she is the teachable type. The people God brings around have lots of wisdom and get financial mentors: business, building, saving. People have specific qualities that can help you too as you watch their lives daily.

Meet people who have the spirit of success in them. The Bible says in Leviticus 26:8*: And five of you shall chase an hundred, and an hundred of you shall put ten thousand to flight.* Jesus explained to us what this meant when He explained praying together in one accord – Matthew 18:20: *For where two or three are gathered together in my name, there am I in the midst of them.* Agreement has to do with reasoning and outlining ways to tackle problems. It is more than just praying. It is more of the thoughtful processing of our heart desires.

The lack of effective financial planning will lead to poverty. When you plan, you will not be like the good man whose vineyard was invaded by the evil one who crept in and sowed tares in the good man's investment while people were sleeping (Matthew 13:25). He was good - someone who had the fear of God - yet his righteousness did not protect his vineyard. Many of us lack the kind of knowledge that will enable us to plan – make money, save money, spend money, invest money, and watch it grow. This is why the Bible says that *a little sleep* – not having plans for your life, and *a little slumber* – no thought of increase, will definitely lead to poverty. Now we may have learned by now that poverty leads to deprivation. We become deprived of joy as we continually hope for someone or God to help us out, and deprived of good health as poor people often soil their environment. Poor people always gossip about other people, engaging their minds in worthless conversation – and this act, we learn, corrupts good manners – 1 Corinthians 15:33. When our good manners are corrupt, where will we get help? God would definitely not be interested in helping the seed of corruption until such seed repents. Corrupt people take bribes and they would destroy the land and lose their inheritance to strangers – Proverbs 29:4: *The king by judgment establisheth the land: but he that receiveth gifts overthroweth it.* This passage explains that by reasoning and wise counsel a king is able to possess his territory, but those who receive bribes would lose all that to strangers. It is difficult to disobey those we take bribes from and that will lead us to losing our sense of reasoning and our wealth. Many of those who are poor expect so much from others, and when they are not getting their heart's desires from those they expect them from, they will begin to mock them, saying things like '*all of us will die someday, where will they take all this money to?*' and you will see many people avoiding them because many display ingratitude from their statements. The Bible says in Proverbs 22:10 NIV: *Drive out the mocker, and out goes strife; quarrels and insults are ended.* This is also the more reason why the rich tend to separate themselves far away from the poor, and will only provide for them to attract the blessings of the Lord upon themselves – Proverbs 22:9 NIV: *A generous man will himself be blessed, for he shares his food with the poor.* Dirty habits, gossiping, disunity amongst the poor and the selfish acts of many poor people are the main reason they don't see increase. I have seen many running after miracles instead of wisdom. Many have failed to realise that they need to confess their sins first before God and obtain salvation before their freedom will come to them as the morning dew. Their impatience is often displayed when they would sell their tomorrow for the sake of having food to eat, as seen when politicians come to demand their votes in exchange for money or bags of grains or other food items – Proverbs 22:7 NIV: *The rich rule over the poor, and the borrower is servant to the lender.*

The poor also expect too much from even their children, to the extent that some would send them into stealing or prostitution, making it difficult sometime for these children to succeed in life against the Bible's advice that *A good man leaves an inheritance for his children's children* – Proverbs 13:22 NIV. And the book of Psalms

112:1-3, says that wealth and riches are in the house of those who fear the Lord.

Why do we have poverty in our midst? The Bible says (Proverbs 22:2): *Rich and poor have this in common: The Lord is the Maker of them all* (NIV). If this is the case, what have the rich learnt that the poor haven't? This is why we are in this discussion, so that we, as the heirs of the kingdom, will have the right thinking perspective – to love and not to hate our fellow human beings.

Two verses of Proverbs 22 struck my mind – verses 4 and 5 (NIV):

- 'Humility and the fear of the Lord bring wealth and honour and life.'
- 'In the paths of the wicked lies thorns and snares, but he who guards his soul stays far from them.'

This means that the reason people cry for want, and why so many who were rich now beg to eat, is because they lacked humility and the fear of the Lord. And because they practised wickedness, thorns and snares, and devourers took away their successes. This is why in Jeremiah 4:3 God advises us not to sow among thorns. This is the spirit of financial planning – knowing when, how, what, where and when to invest.

CHAPTER EIGHT

THE CHARACTER OF A FINANCIAL PLANNER

We are advised in Psalms 112:5: *A good man sheweth favour, and lendeth: he will guide his affairs with discretion.* Now that we understand the reason why we must plan financially so as to escape from the snare of financial slavery, let's take a careful look into our earlier verse: *A prudent man sees danger and takes refuge, but the simple keep going and suffer for it* (NIV) – Proverbs 22:3. From here we would extract the character of an effective financial planner:

- **Prudent:** He or she is not prodigal in spending and abhors wasting money on impulsive buying and unnecessary engagement in merriments. Such a person is very practical and does not build castles in the air. They don't like playing to the gallery, but are sincere about their financial status. In teaching my young ones this quality, I often advise anyone close to me to have a bank account first. This is where prudence starts from – making savings, no matter how small. The book of Job 8:7 says: *Though thy beginning was small, yet thy latter end should greatly increase.* Those who despise the mustard seed kind of beginning will not make headway in investment.

- **Alert:** He or she is very careful about the future. They know when to invest and when not. They read the failure and success stories of others and will use them to fine-tune their plans, and not as an excuse not to venture out into the deep ocean of investment.
- **Knowledge of tomorrow:** As a financial planner someone is aware of what tomorrow will bring by studying the economy and government policy. They study the yearly budget of the nation and area of operation and see how it will affect their investments or savings. They also study the world economy and how other nations are surviving. This was the reason Jacob had to go to Egypt. And God also told Abraham to see ahead of him. Jesus also opens our understanding into the events of the last days. A financial planner is forward-thinking in his actions. He doesn't finish all he has today - he thinks of tomorrow.

- **A thought for a rainy day:** Planning ensures that much is saved for tomorrow. This is where you know a wise fellow – Proverbs 21:20 NIV: *In the house of the wise are stores of choice food and oil, but a foolish man devours all he has.* He or she saves for a rainy day. In time of scarcity, the good financial planner will still have enough in stock and will not be hit by inflated prices of goods. This is the 'wisdom of Joseph' in Egypt at work here.
- **Patient:** A great word of admonition came from our Lord on how patience can preserve our soul when He said: *In your patience possess ye your souls* – Luke 21:19. This would mean that those who are patient and waiting on the Lord's season of visitation as Solomon did will make wealth and will not lose their soul to the devil.
- **Humility:** I got a word of knowledge from the Lord sometime ago while I battled with knowing what qualities I needed to know those who would work with me to do the work the Lord had apportioned to me. He said – all you need are people who are *extremely humble and available.* With this criterion, it wasn't hard for me to carry out a winnowing exercise, knowing who to entrust with certain responsibilities.

This was how God selected soldiers for Gideon too in Judges 7:2-7. In the Gideon story, the first sets were afraid because they didn't see the possibility of God helping them to achieve the vision of deliverance and peace ahead. The second set couldn't lap water with their tongues, meaning they are the sets of people who are difficult to train in accepting new ways of doing things right as they are stuck to their zones of comfort. What we just discussed is a test of humility. When we are humble, we tell ourselves the truth and seek avenues to make up for the deficiency we have. A humble person is one who seeks God, and sacrifices to serve Him. A financial planner is a humble person. The proud is improvident too.

- **Decisive:** A decisive person keeps his tongue in his cheek and his word in his palm. He has foresight and is willing to go against the popular decision of the crowd, provided it will bring glory to God, as David did when he defeated Goliath. Those who set the stage for tomorrow are those who make their decision to succeed today. There is no one under the influence of the Spirit of God that is not decisive - if not, what is the usefulness of hearing God's voice behind leading us on the path to follow?

- **Diligent:** We can find wisdom relating to this in Proverbs 22:29: *Seest thou a man diligent in his business? he shall stand before kings; he shall not stand before mean men.* A diligent person gives you his word, and stands to defend every letter in the word as he carries out his work daily. They are not good at procrastination. They are industrious and do not covet their neighbours' wealth. When they have a wealthy relative, they will not try seeing him as their benefactor, but they strive to see how they can even assist their wealthy relative to become even wealthier. They do not loot the national treasury when in government to solve their problems, but will see how they can leave their godly exploits behind in the sands of time for others to emulate. A diligent wife will make her husband happy and fulfilled by spending wisely. A diligent employee will make a happy employer. A diligent believer is a blessing unto soul-winning campaigns. Diligence brings honour. This is the torchlight we are admonished to bear for all to see, so that they can glorify God in heaven – Matthew 5:16.
- **Articulate:** An articulate person is one with good eloquent speech. Such oratory skill is good in negotiating business terms. This is what often distinguishes the wise from the foolish investor.

Proverbs 18:20 says: *A man's belly shall be satisfied with the fruit of his mouth; and with the increase of his lips shall he be filled.* What we shall eat tomorrow depends on what we say with our mouths today – Proverbs 15:23: *A man hath joy by the answer of his mouth: and a word spoken in due season, how good is it.* You don't need all the wisdom now; it is only that which is meaningful to the situation at hand.

- **Good sleeping habits:** You need good mental focus to manage wealth. When the Bible made mention of a little sleep and a little slumber, what is meant is not physical sleep, but nonchalance. When you are dispassionate about what you are doing, you lose control over it. You can't plan what you do not have control over. It is good to take your sleep as required so that you won't become dizzy during a board meeting. That would show unseriousness on your part, and everyone working with you will toe that line.
- **Spiritual:** The fear of the Lord is the beginning of wisdom, so we are informed in Proverbs 9:10. Our spiritual relevance starts when we fear the Lord, and then we are able to keep His commands so that our wealth-seeking efforts will not hit the rocks.

These qualities culminate in the spirit of survival you see

in those with the spirit to make life work. This is why they often seek spiritual help that will enable them to see into the future. Many however are led astray, as they would sell their souls to the devil and be cast into the den of the devil. The Bible says (Proverbs 21:31): *The horse is made ready for the day of battle, but victory rests with the Lord* (NIV). This is advice for those who prefer to sleep, dying in the church, all in the name of praying for success when they are not yet prepared to set out. We must set our plans and desires in place through effective strategic preparedness before God can move into action.

How do you know that you are planning? Action they say speaks louder than words. Jesus opens our understanding to this – Matthew 11:4-5: ... *Go and shew John again those things which ye do hear and see: The blind receive their sight, and the lame walk, the lepers are cleansed, and the deaf hear, the dead are raised up, and the poor have the gospel preached to them.* It is a 'show me' affair. Where is the evidence to show that you have the character to succeed in life?

CHAPTER NINE

THE ENEMIES OF FINANCIAL PLANNING

The main benefit of financial planning is that it helps us to minimize waste. Time and resources remain the most observable elements of waste. Just as long as Gideon was unable to move forward until God selected his soldiers, so also we would remain stagnant until we plan financially. For Gideon, his burden would include feeding and medical care for the soldiers, and they have to conquer their enemies in a timely manner. With God's planning, the wasteful resources that would have been invested on 32,000 soldiers were reduced to cater for only a needful 300 men. When the Israelites were fed from heaven with manna, God made it known that they should not waste. When Jesus taught us how to pray, He said we should only ask for daily bread. After feeding the five thousand, He said the disciples should gather the remnant. Now that we understand these elements of waste, we also need to know what leads to waste. This includes:

- **Indecision:** If we look at the character of God, we see that God is firm in His decisions. On the other hand, the devil moves to and fro and therefore is not firm in his decisions. Once we are afraid of failure, there is no way we can be decisive. The Bible says: *He that observeth the wind shall not sow; and he that regardeth the clouds shall not reap* – Ecclesiastes 11:4. Sometimes, when people think they are being thorough in their lives, which they would say is the reason they are not coming up with a decision on what to do, a look at their actions will point to the fact that they are afraid of failure or people's judgment of their actions. Such people hardly make ends meet. God looked at the world and there was darkness, and He moved into action to correct the anomaly He saw. Then he separated the waste - darkness - from the product, light. Decision is a winnowing effort and only those who are realistic in life can be decisive. They often go against the crowd to put the facts across in a productive manner.

- **Procrastination:** Those who procrastinate never get to their destinations on time. Though they finally get there, they are often left with regrets - 'had I known.' They consume their tomorrow today and would plan their today tomorrow. They are not proactive in nature. Their hearts are filled with momentary merriment, which is devoid of savings.
- **Wild investment:** The parable of the sower teaches us what I am explaining here (Matthew 13). Why did the sower sow in lands that were not fertile? The answer would be lack of investment planning, and he wasted his seeds, reducing his income. Sowing without effective planning leads to waste. This is the beauty of wisdom. The Bible says in Ecclesiastes 10:2: *A wise man's heart is at his right hand; but a fool's heart at his left.* Meaning that a wise man's investment or treasure, represented here as 'heart,' is guided by wisdom (right hand), while the fool invests without an element of wisdom. The success of our sowing effort is guided by how much attention we give to it – Matthew 6:21: *For where your treasure is, there will your heart be also.* When we sow successfully, and the increase begins to manifest, we will have enough to bring out to support the work of God – Matthew 12:34: *A good man out of the good treasure of the heart bringeth forth-good things.* And to ensure that we don't

sow amiss, we need to be serious with our planning, and the implementation of what we had planned. There is no idleness in the Kingdom of God – Matthew 12:36: *But I say unto you, that every idle word that men shall speak, they shall give account thereof in the Day of Judgment*. Why? Because the time you spend speaking idle words should have been invested. If you have nothing to do, win a soul. If you are still bored, pick up a book on a profession and read. If you still need more, read my books and I bet you you will be filled with wisdom. If all these fail you, then grab the Bible, and prayerfully read through the word of God. You won't regret the time you have invested, and the Lord will be proud of you. How about that?

- **Irony of the Pond:** It is believed that as long as there is water in the pond there are always fish in it, until it is emptied. It is this expectation that encourages the pond owner to want to drain the water down until the pond bed is seen. In some cases, holes dug around the walls of the pond are exposed to see if a fish could be hiding there. Many of us waste our money because we feel there is still enough until finally it dawns on us that we had no savings. Expecting too much from our investments will make us waste what we have now. I have seen salary earners use all their earnings before the end of the month, expecting more the next month. This attitude will not enable one to invest continuously. This leads to procrastination, because we assume that tomorrow will be better than today. It is this foolishness that is seen displayed by most believers. And one may notice this attitude in their prayers too. This is why in Ecclesiastes 10:7 the Bible says: *I have seen servants upon horses, and princes walking as servants upon the earth.* The servants saved their meagre rewards, as they had no inheritance, while the princes squandered their inheritance because they felt it would never end. This verse of the Bible is very dear to my heart, because I have experienced deprivation in life before, so I wouldn't want to be there again.

- **Misplaced Priority:** What is a misplaced priority? Let's get an understanding from what Jesus says of the wine skin – Luke 5:38: *But new wine must be put into new bottles; and both are preserved.* He advised that we should put new wine into a new wine skin. Why should someone save money for a project that is yet to commence, which will still take a long while, instead of investing the money to yield more profit now? Some people have taken loans from the bank for their marriage ceremonies, waiting for people to donate to them so that they can offset their bills, and then they are disappointed when those they expected fail to turn up for the wedding or send gifts later. Someone sent me a text message some time ago that he was disappointed in me because I didn't even send a gift for his wedding, and what came to my mind was that on my wedding day I didn't get any gift. Why should that bother me? I don't live on other peoples' wallets. I mind my own wallet, so why should someone be interested in what is in mine? This is the spirit of greed and covetousness, which as I said earlier are determining factors for failure in life. Some wedding cards are too expensive. Many have actually become poor after seeing so much wealth as a result of misplaced priorities. Some politicians and business owners have travelled overseas to celebrate birthdays for their concubines. There are also many men who live in Nigeria, for instance, whose wives and families are abroad, doing nothing productive there, and the man has to fly abroad every now and then to see his family. Many such women have actually become wives to other young men out there, draining the man's income. What is more important? Is it the family staying together in joy, or the feeling that one's family stays abroad? I have seen many who retire with nothing to show for their hard work, having laboured under the sun due to misplaced priorities. Some invested in cars whose value depreciates the moment you drive it out of the showroom. Many women invest in gold wristwatches and jewellery, and these have been stolen by armed robbers, in some cases.

- **Pride:** Many do not see their pride until they fall into a big pit. Most of the denials we get from people are as a result of our pride. When pride sets in, our thoughts are submerged in self-praise. The more we live in self-praise, the more we grow stale in our thoughts. The Bible says (Ecclesiastes 10:1): *Dead flies cause the ointment of the apothecary to send forth a stinking savour: so doth a little folly him that is in reputation for wisdom and honour.* This explains that the misbehaviour of someone held in high esteem is unpardonable by the public. A pastor dies in pride when he thinks that he is above all and therefore does not need advice. A wise man knows which advice to take and which to jettison. When I wasn't taking financial spending advice from my wife, I made the worst financial blunders of my life, but when I allowed her into my reasoning, I understood that two good heads are indeed better than one. When I finally allow God in and continually reasoned with Him, that was when I received a leap in life. There is someone out there who is better than you in reasoning - meet him for advice. Don't lock up yourself in pride; grow the kind of wings that you can fold in when the need arises.

- **Gambling:** Gamblers expect too much from tomorrow. They believe that by throwing in a coin into a casino machine, they will reap millions as a jackpot. It is also those with this kind of heart that look for miracle prayer as if it is a scarce commodity. When the devil came to tempt Jesus, what he wanted Jesus to do was gamble, until Jesus disappointed him. Telling Jesus to change stone to bread was gambling. Jumping from the pinnacle of the temple is gambling with one's life. Bowing down to worship the devil, all in the promise of gaining the whole world, is gambling. How many of us have fallen for the devil's trick of gambling? Changing your age to get a job is gambling, just as Esau gambled with his age, and lost eternity. Prostitution is gambling. Cheating in an exam hall is gambling. Stealing is gambling. No one who gambles can be a successful financial planner. The Oxford Dictionary of English defines gambling, as 'taking a risky action in the hope of a desired result'. Whatever becomes risky can become an avenue for poverty and the loss of self-esteem. Be cautious!
- **Inexperience:** Getting the services of inexperienced people can make us waste valuable time and resources. We often do business with the wrong people. In Nigeria such an investment is termed 'Money miss road.' We can only get the help of

experienced people when we know what we are looking for, and then drive to see it materialise through employing divine wisdom.

- **Poverty mentality:** The problem with poverty is not the lack of money; it is the lack of up-to-date knowledge about a particular aspect of life. For instance, I may be rich financially, but poor in education. This educational poverty will drive its fangs into the lifeblood of our investment later as the day grows, and then we will have deadly venom devouring our intentions to deal with. This is a time when a crucial decision is needed to save a situation at the material time, and we will discover that the information needed is missing, and the means to acquiring it is also eluding everyone present or within call. Poverty mentality is pride activated. A heart filled with pride will never want to seek knowledge. The Bible says in Hosea 4:6, that suffering is a product of lack of cognate knowledge. So we can say that poverty mentality sets in first as information deprivation, and then grows into an inferiority complex. This with time will degenerate into hatred for others who are better than you, and then you will discover that you are getting boxed in, with no freedom to exercise your goals in life. As this happens, you would begin to see every successful person as your enemy. Then you will see yourself cursing the rich and those in authority, against the Bible's warning in Ecclesiastes 10:20: *Curse not the king, no not in thy thought; and curse not the rich in thy bedchamber: for a bird of the air shall carry the voice, and that which hath wings shall tell the matter.* Then, just as we just read, the hatred you have created will begin to create a cloud of seclusion around you, and whatever you do will also inherit that seclusion – your employment, your business and your entire life, so that when you are in need, the spirit of seclusion will separate you from those who would have helped you, and rather, you will only see those who will come and hiss, and give you a comfort of mockery.

- **Greed:** I have decided to talk about greed separately, though it is an innate habit present in those who gamble. Greed is defined by the Oxford Dictionary of English as 'intense and selfish desire for something, especially wealth, power, or food'. The problem is not the desire, but the adjectival clause, 'intense and selfish', expressing the manner in which wealth, power or food are desired by greedy people. Does this explain why greed is in the hearts of so many people – intense desire for wealth, power or food? Such a person is *as death, and cannot be satisfied* – Habakkuk 2:5. A greedy person is also a deceitful one – 2 Peter 2:3: *And through covetousness shall they with feigned words make merchandise of you: whose judgment now of a long time* *lingereth not, and their damnation slumbereth not.* Anyone with the spirit of greed does not have insight into the future. There is no way one can plan financially without having tomorrow in mind.

- **Stealing**: Jesus says – John 10:1: *Verily, verily, I say unto you, He that entereth not by the door into the sheepfold, but climbeth up some other way, the same is a thief and a robber.* Thieves break into houses impatiently to steal. Anyone who is impatient will definitely not be a good financial planner. Those who steal are also murderers, idol worshippers, adulterers and adulteresses, etc. – Jeremiah 7:9: *Will ye steal, murder, and commit adultery, and swear falsely, and burn incense unto Baal, and walk after other gods whom ye know not.* A thief is also under the curse of God, and no one under a curse will also plan effectively – Zechariah 5:4: *I will bring it forth, saith the Lord of hosts, and it shall enter into the house of the thief, and into the house of him that sweareth falsely by my name: and it shall remain in the midst of his house, and shall consume it with the timber thereof and the stones thereof.*

- **Economic and Political Factors:** Inflation, hyperinflation, bank lending rates, unemployment, war, etc are all enemies of financial planning. This is why business investors are very careful to invest in war-torn environments. All over the world, wherever war is, the economy collapses.

- **Not Sowing:** We are informed: *In the morning sow thy seed, and in the evening withhold not thine hand: for thou knowest not whether shall prosper, either this or that, or whether they both shall be alike good* – Ecclesiastes 11:6. We sow in the morning, and also provide for those in need who have come to labour in our investments in the evening after the day's job, so that they can have dinner to eat. People who don't have the habit of continual investment are also poor financial planners. The Bible admonishes us in Proverbs 28:19: *He that tilleth his land shall have plenty of bread: but he that followeth after vain persons shall have poverty enough.* I sow spiritually and physically. Sowing includes the assistance we render to others. It involves the show of goodwill when we are opportune – this is the essence of love. You cannot tell how far your 'goodwill' has gone until you are in need. If you have a generous heart, someone will be generous to you. If you have not groped to find a matchbox to light your candle in the night, you won't know what it feels like to be in need of help. The Lord advised thus – Matthew 5:7: *Blessed are the merciful: for they shall obtain mercy.* It is a popular saying that 'one good turn deserves another'. Therefore, one good sowing deserves another. The more the sowing, the more the expectation of increase.

Jesus says that we have the poor with us always (Matthew 26:11). There is no minister of the word of God who does not plan with the poor in their midst. If we were to build a house of worship for the successful-only in society, there would be no need for massive cathedrals. We can borrow a leaf from this to ask ourselves what do we have with us always. This is what we need to plan with. What many of us do is to plan with what we cannot lay our hands on, and such planning always starts with, "when." For instance, a procrastinating fellow would make statements such as "when I get a job I will start to think of buying a car." In most cases a fellow like this who doesn't have a good planning habit ends up not studying the market, so they end up wasting more money on few items. Those who know the benefits that come with wealth and riches will always seek the knowledge of financial planning. But before we go ahead to the next chapter to learn the wisdom of investment, let us see a portion of the Bible which tells us what we need to do to have wealth and riches that would stand the test of time so that all our financial planning efforts will not be lost in the sea of illusion. And that portion is Psalms 112, and I am quoting from the NIV:

1 *Praise the Lord. Blessed is the man who fears the Lord, who finds great delight in his commands.*

2 *His children will be mighty in the land; the generation of the upright will be blessed.*

3 *Wealth and riches are in his house, and his righteousness endures forever.*

4 *Even in darkness light dawns for the upright, for the gracious and compassionate and righteous man.*

5 *Good will come to him who is generous and lends freely, who conducts his affairs with justice.*

6 *Surely he will never be shaken; a righteous man will be remembered forever.*

7 *He will have no fear of bad news; his heart is steadfast, trusting in the Lord.*

8 *His heart is secure, he will have no fear; in the end he will look in triumph on his foes.*

9 *He has scattered abroad his gifts to the poor, his righteousness endures forever; his horn will be lifted high in honour.*

10 *The wicked man will see and be vexed, he will gnash his teeth and waste away; the longings of the wicked will come to nothing.*

CHAPTER TEN

WISDOM FOR INVESTMENT

Let's see the advice of Joseph to the Egyptians in Genesis 47:23-24: *Then Joseph said unto the people, Behold, I have bought you this day and your land for Pharaoh: lo, here is seed for you, and ye shall sow the land. And it shall come to pass in the increase, that ye shall give the fifth part unto Pharaoh, and four parts shall be your own, for seed of the field, and for your food, and for them of your households, and for food for your little ones.* We will now draw on this advice to help us also sustain our lives. The people were Pharaoh's properties and as such Pharaoh gives them land and seed to sow and in return they are to give one fifth of the harvest to the household of Pharaoh, so that he can take care of all those helping him to administer Egypt. We have been bought by Christ, and

He has also given us wisdom to make wealth and as a mark of loyalty we are supposed to make returns. If we follow Joseph's arithmetic, that would be giving 20% to the work of God from your earnings, if truly you believe that the Lord is behind your increase. From the remaining four fifths or 80%, they would store for re-investment, use for food and cater for those in their home, including servants, and for the children. With this at the back of our minds, we are set to invest. Lets hit the road.

I was about to start speculative stock trading when I read in a book: 'if you know you will regret this money you are about to invest when the stock value drops, then don't proceed'. This was why I did not proceed. Before you go into investments, please seek advice. I bought some land some time ago and I have lost all, because I got them from fraudulent people. Many people have retired and those who duped them took their retirement benefits from them. There are criminals who disguise themselves as rendering a helping hand when you are in need to set up an investments. There are fraudulent people out there waiting for your money. Just be cautious.

There are verses in the Bible that talk about investment:

- **Genesis 33:18:** *And Jacob came to Shalem, a city of Shechem, which is in the land of Canaan, when he came from Padanaram; and pitched his tent before the* *city. And he bought a parcel of a field, where he had spread his tent, at the hand of the children of Hamor, Shechem's father, for an hundred pieces of money.* No matter what, even if a friend is trying to offer you a land for free, learn from Jacob's instance above and Abraham in Genesis 23:9-16 – always pay the full price. People offer help in disguise and when you have invested, the devil will enter into their hearts and they will demand their land back. Which means you will have to uproot your investment. Be careful, *the heart (of man) is deceitful above all things, and desperately wicked: who can know it?* – Jeremiah 17:9. Seal every investment with a deal duly signed, even if it is with your father, mother, spouse, child, trusted friend, pastor, etc., because when it comes to money the devil can use anyone to upturn a gentleman's agreement.

- **Genesis 47:20:** *And Joseph bought all the land of Egypt for Pharaoh; for the Egyptians sold every man his field, because the famine prevailed over them: so the land became Pharaoh's.* Save money for the 'opportunity day' when what would normally cost a million dollars may go for a few hundred dollars. Use your instincts guided by the wisdom of God – you need it to invest.

- **Leviticus 27:22:** *And if a man sanctify unto the Lord a field which he hath bought, which is not of the fields of his possession.* You can also buy land and sanctify it unto the work of God, releasing it to the service of the Lord. This is spiritual investment. We can also see this in 2 Samuel 24:21: *And David said, To buy the threshingfloor of thee, to build an altar unto the Lord.* Consider investing in the Kingdom of God. The Altar will speak in your favour as long as you are still bonded to the Lord's service.
- **Jeremiah 32:9:** *And I (Jeremiah) bought the field of Hanameel my uncle's son, that was in Anathoth, and weighed him the money, even seventeen shekels of silver.* A servant of God too can invest in properties.
- **Proverbs 31:15:** *She considereth a field, and buyeth it: with the fruit of her hands she planteth a vineyard.* This is a key ingredient in investment – consider and make research before investing. Limit borrowing and invest with your own money. Don't let the investment go fallow – plant something into it that will grow and become economically viable. Better still, rent it out to one who would pay you in money and not in kind. Remember, this is business.

As a child of God, your exploits are supposed to make the wicked bitter. If you don't increase, how will they go bitter and would want to seek your God? This is wisdom for the soul. We would be seeing some wisdom to help us invest our money below.

- **Early retirement:** If you are working for an establishment, and you want to pursue investment, there is every possibility that those who would manage the business for you may run you aground. This is why you need to consider the option of retiring from your place of work early. And again, you may also want to retire from active business, to become a CEO, while you employ the services of trusted fellows to help you manage the business. Be mindful of employing the services of an unfaithful fellow, because when the chips are down, you won't see him to give accurate accounts – Proverbs 25:29: *Confidence in an unfaithful man in time of trouble is like a broken tooth, and a foot out of joint.* It is all about how you view it and how much sincere risk you are willing to cope with.
- **Reduce borrowing:** Even if you are going to borrow to run your business, be careful not to have so much borrowed money in your hands that it is not working

for you. The act of borrowing can increase one's anxiety, when there is loss in business and we become restless for this reason – Proverbs 22:7: ... *the borrower is servant to the lender.* The Bible sees non-payment of the loans we borrow as an act of wickedness - Psalm 37:21: *The wicked borroweth, and payeth not again.* So we must ensure that we borrow only what we are sure we can pay. For this reason we are also admonished not to owe anyone - Romans 13:8: *Owe no man any thing.*

- **Be serious minded:** If you are not serious with what you do, people won't take you seriously. Jesus gave us a clue to this when He spoke about John the Baptist in Matthew 11:7-9,11. John wasn't a reed that was shaken by wind, meaning he was firm. He wasn't dressing like one set out for leisure; he was more than a prophet, and so he was dressed as one. Don't forget that many who would meet you may want to run down your ideas, not because they aren't good, but because they want to let you know that they have superior ideas to yours, and if you are not careful, you may start harbouring the thoughts of an inferiority complex within you. These kinds of people behave like the buyer who, to try to get a product at a lower price, may say the product is not exactly what he wanted – Proverbs 20:14: *It is naught, it is naught, saith the buyer: but when he is gone his way, then he boasteth.* Those who mean well don't run you down, they rather encourage you and chip in some very productive advice referred to as productive critique. Be careful not to always run to the same person for advice – they may have run out of advice, but to meet your expectations they may have to cook up counsel for you. This is often the problem with some prophets – they don't have the information, but they have to give advice to enable them to sustain your patronage.

- **Count your loss:** People always talk of counting our blessings and naming them one by one as a way of knowing how much the Lord has blessed us. In financial planning terms, it is more advisable to count your loss, so that you will apply caution on time. In Proverbs 31:18, we see that the virtuous woman actually reviewed her investment to be able to know how valuable they are - *She perceiveth that her merchandise is good: her candle goeth not out by night.* A principle you would see here also is dedication – her light doesn't go out at night. Why? In the evenings people return home from their workplaces to buy items. The more you count your loss, the more you understand other factors that affect investment timing. Seasons and times affect your investment. Investing in cold beverages is better during the hot season of the year. Umbrellas will sell better in the wet season. You have your opportunity, now use it well – remember the saying that opportunity comes but once. The Bible advises also in Proverbs 27:23: *Be thou diligent to know the state of thy flocks, and look well to thy herds. For riches are not for ever: and doth the crown endure to every generation.* Counting your loss requires diligence. To be diligent is to be persistent. It involves asking and knowing.

- **Bind your investment with a spiritual oath:** The Bible advises (Proverbs 3:9): *Honour the Lord with thy substance, and with the firstfruits of all thine increase: So shall thy barns be filled with plenty, and thy presses shall burst out with new wine.* There is always a spiritual oath that protects every successful business. First anyone that will work with you, including yourself, prays because there is a spiritual being you and they want to connect with every time. And because humans are often controlled by various spiritual invocations, if you fail to bind your business to an altar of the Lord, there is every tendency that you will be experiencing loss as the devil sits down in your investment by using those he has possessed to make decisions that will lead to your downfall. Ephesians 6:12 says that humans are in a spiritual wrestling match with powers in high places. If your business does not have a spiritual flavour that connects it to the realm of God, be sure to have policies made by those principalities in power, through their agents in government, and such policies will never favour your investment. In some cases, these policies are made when you have just taken a loan to increase your reach, and maybe you are becoming a competitor with one of theirs. This is why the Bible says that the people rejoice when the righteous rule. Having devil-induced wicked individuals at the helm of affairs will always spell doom for God's children, unless they plead to the Lord to intervene. Tithes and offerings bind your business to the altar. Tithe is a holy seed that is meant to be returned to the altar to be eating by those who work in the holy place. A deep spiritual secret is revealed concerning the sacredness of the tenth part in Isaiah 6:8-13: *Also I heard the voice of the Lord, saying ...* ***But yet in it shall be a tenth, and it shall return, and shall be eaten****: as a teil tree, and as an oak, whose substance is in them, when they cast their leaves****: so the holy seed shall be the substance thereof.*** Take a look again at the highlighted revelations. Don't forget that this was the Lord still talking from verse 8 of this Bible passage. This is how we get spiritual codes and use them to better our lives. There is a spiritual substance of increase in the tenth portion of your income, and when you return it to God it becomes a Holy Seed that will yield its spiritual substance for you to become established. Your relationship with the servant of God must be cordial, with a spiritual tone, if you want to make it in business. I have heard stories of some business owners even making some servants of God shareholders in their investment. Just act as you are led spiritually. The Lord wants you to remember Him in everything, because He owns you and your investments, and this is why we pay tithes and offerings and make vows of faithfulness before Him. Hear His complaint in Isaiah 1:3: *The ox knoweth his owner, and the ass his master's crib: but Israel doth not know, my people doth not consider.* If God owns you, you cannot deny Him anything, not even your life. Anyone following the Lord should have the heart and mind of Queen Esther – *if I perish, I perish* – Esther 4:16. Bind yourself, your marriage, your children and your investments to the altar of the Lord, be faithful thereafter to the payment of commitments financially and otherwise, and see the Lord's arm in your entrepreneurial pursuits.

- **Investing in agriculture:** If you must invest in agriculture – crops, trees, animal husbandry, etc., you must know that these have life and they can die at any time. Natural disasters can sweep them away. Pests and diseases can infect them; this is why you need experts' advice. You can hire the services of a professional in the area of interest, or better still, enrol under someone who is already successful for tutelage. Some have also sought employment to work in such places, before venturing out. You can also visit the government ministry of agriculture and see if there are incentives the government is giving to the famers. We also have agricultural banks that give soft loans to farmers. You must understand the use of fertilizers too. Job invested in agriculture, and we see this evidence in Job 1:14-16. Abraham also had plenty of livestock. Isaac and Jacob also invested their time in rearing animals. The evidence is there for all to see in the book of Genesis. To succeed, you must buy a piece of land or rent one. I don't really advise renting land – outright buying is more profitable in the long run. When the Lord led the Israelites out of Egypt, He led them into Canaan, an agriculturally rich land. The word, 'flowing with milk and honey,' expressed the richness of food in the land. Honey and milk are products from agricultural investments.

- **Investing in the Stock Market:** Here is where you would want to apply caution; the fluidity of the stock market is hard to predict because it depends on many factors. The business environment must be favourable for stocks to grow. You must monitor the political scenery before you proceed and be one who reads and can interpret market trends, even if you engage the services of stockbrokers. Buy books on stock trading before venturing out.

- **Forex Trading:** I have seen many people succeed here and have also seen others who have lost, to the extent of attempting suicide. But it is worth trying provided you are well informed and you have a trusted consultant to advise you. Make a search of some materials you could lay your hands on and read online. You may also want to try out some videos on YouTube before finally venturing into it. Your bank manager can also help you out here. In all, it is all about whom you trust enough to take their financial investment advice.

- **Selling of goods and services:** I went into a supermarket one day, only to discover that the sell-by dates of most of the goods had expired. This is the fate of most supermarkets, especially when they are located where sales are poor. This is the reason why many set a business up in busy areas where you have the high income spenders living. If you want to invest in the supply of services, target the rich as customers, and if you must sustain their patronage, fill your shop with what attracts ladies and children. If you want to service industry, then you need real capital to set out. Get advice from your bank manager, and attend conferences, workshops etc relating to the area of service you want to offer.
- **Investing in property:** Investing in property is wonderful provided you are dealing with genuine agents. Do study a great deal of information on the

Internet first. It is available and free. Google for all the available information on property investment before approaching your bank for advice. Only after you are done with your bank should you consider meeting a property agent. Though many property agents may be trusted, there are also many who are fraudulent.

- **Investing in minerals:** To me this is the most security challenging investment, because this is where all the wicked businessmen who have sold their soul to the devil want to invest. Government interest here is also very high. This doesn't mean it is not worth considering. If you see it you will get it. If this is your vision, with the help of the Lord, all things are possible. The Bible says – Deuteronomy 32:13: *He made him ride on the high places of the earth, that he might eat the increase of the fields; and he made him to suck honey out of the rock, and oil out of the flinty rock.* Jacob was counted among the nobles of his days, and I am very sure he superseded them. The Lord did this for him so that he would eat the increase of his investment. Jacob got oil out of the flinty rock – this is a mineral. We have read how precious stones were used in the building of the tabernacle. How did these minerals come without exploration?

- **Investing in education:** This is very important, especially with knowledge increasing these days in fulfilment of Daniel's prophecy – Daniel 12:4: *Many shall run to and fro, and knowledge shall increase* (ESV). Academic training is demanding and needs to be carefully thought through before proceeding. Whether you own an educational establishment or you are enrolling to be trained in specific professions, it all requires money. If you want to own an educational outfit you have to consider quality of delivery, security, location and accessibility, and availability of funds to run it in the beginning. You would have to buy a landed property too. Renting a property to run a school may only be beneficial at the outset. The property owner may become jealous and want to take over his property to set up another business or even start a school himself. See advice on the necessary registration processes. Get expert advice too, perhaps from the ministry of education.

These suggestions are not exhaustive; you can find a great deal of information if you seek it from the professionals – Proverbs 15:22: *Without counsel purposes are disappointed: but in the multitude of counsellors they are established.* In all, as a child of God, be careful not to be involved in ungodly deeds, else the day the Lord visits your establishment, everything that offends Him will be taken away with the wind of sanctification – Matthew 10:16: *Behold, I send you forth as sheep in the midst of wolves: be ye therefore wise as serpents, and harmless as doves.* Never join evil – as a believer, let your light so shine – Matthew 5:16. Be an example to fraudulent investors so that they will follow you to the house of the Lord, to learn His ways – Zechariah 8:23, Isaiah 2:3.

Investment opportunities are like beautiful virgins, so you must mind how you lust after them – they are capital intensive, and have the power to break your heart. The Bible cautioned (Proverbs 6:25): *Lust not after her beauty in thine heart; neither let her take thee with her eyelids.* It is not all that glitters that is gold. We must be careful with what entices us. It is not all business that is productive and pleasing to the Lord. For instance, running a brothel is against the dignity of man and the will of God, so it is not an attractive business. In Matthew 13:44 we have a cluc of what we should invest in – the field must have a treasure - *Again, the kingdom of heaven is like unto treasure hid in a field; the which when a man hath found, he hideth, and for joy thereof goeth and selleth all that he hath, and buyeth that field.* This is an investment clue before our eyes – sell the non-profitable business and invest the money in a more profitable one. Later we will come to know this reality of scouting for investment opportunities. In my book *Understand Your Destiny*, I wrote that we need to **Scout** for opportunities, **Invest** in the opportunity, **Monitor** the investment, **Review** your performance, and make **Amend** as required **(SIMRA).** We read earlier in Ecclesiastes 11:4 that *He that observeth the wind shall not sow; and he that regardeth the clouds shall not reap.* Those who are making excuses that they couldn't invest because the business terrain wasn't stable are not wise. There are opportunities that the unstable environment still favours. For instance, with the advent of ebola virus disease (EVD), those who manufacture hand sanitizers were laughing all the way to the bank. Other personal hygiene product manufacturers also made profits. There is something in vogue right now – search for it, if it is sin in disguise, then avoid it. We are told that anyone who is lazy perishes - Proverbs 21:5: *The desire of the slothful killeth him; for his hands refuse to labour.* The reason is because lazy people have all the excuses to give as the reason why they are not making financial gains – 'there was rain, no one to help me, I didn't wake up early, there was a hold up, etc.'

The Lord had heaven, yet He still came down to Earth to invest, and the result of that was (1 Corinthians 10:26): *For the earth is the Lord's, and the fulness thereof.* Even the devil is investing on the face of the Earth. Get employed by the Lord to oversee one of His large estates. You wont regret it. Know the right people to discuss your investment idea with – know the 'who' behind every opportunity and what you can discuss with them. Jesus once gave an instance of this when He warned – Matthew 7:6: *Give not that which is holy unto the dogs, neither cast ye your pearls before swine, lest they trample them under their feet, and turn again and rend you.* Your spouse may not be the right person to discuss your idea with, nor will it always be your brother. Your gatekeeper may even be in a better position at that material time to offer you better advice. Seek the Lord always and always – Be Wise! Tune to the 'How Do They Do It?' and 'How it's Made' Programs on Discovery TV channel and you will be glad you did. People are out there doing something. Ask how do they do it, and you will start doing something.

I would recommend you get my book *How Good and Large is Your Land* [2] as another helpful guide as you soar through the world of investment decision-making.

CHAPTER ELEVEN

STAGES OF FINANCIAL PLANNING

It is advised that at every point in time one should be at alert to one's financial spending and involvement. I usually do this yearly. Right from the day I had this understanding, prudence has lived in my heart. My life received a wonderful transformation when I studied the book of Proverbs 6:6–11: *Go to the ant, O sluggard; consider her ways, and be wise. Without having any chief, officer, or ruler, she prepares her bread in summer and gathers her food in harvest. How long will you lie there, O sluggard? When will you arise from your sleep? A little sleep, a little slumber, a little folding of the hands to rest, and poverty will come upon you like a robber, and want like an armed man* (ESV). This portion of the Bible summarise the reason for financial planning. One must make hay while the sun shines, seek knowledge for guidance, and burn the midnight oil thinking. The last verse we read above left me wondering – and I understood why those who steal and cheat others to earn a living soon become poor. The Bible says that those who perpetrate the act of cheating and stealing are an offence unto God – Proverbs 20:23: *Divers weights are an abomination unto the Lord; and a false balance is not good.* Those who adjust fuel-dispensing meters for much gain, and those who take away grain from the original sacks and reseal them thereafter so that they can make more profit, are all an abomination unto the Lord.

In this chapter, we will be discussing the stages of the financial planning process. This discussion is not exhaustive, but I have decided to talk about it as an appetiser to whet your thoughts so that you become hungry for more information on financial planning stages. The importance of information cannot be overemphasizing when we start planning, so I would advise that all the information you have been gathering since you started reading this book should be laid on the table now. In effect the more information you have, the more it is possible for you to make a humble and wise decision - Proverbs 22:20 says: *Have I not written for you thirty sayings of counsel and knowledge, to make you know what is right and true, that you may give a true answer to those who sent you* (ESV). If you want to be an effective money planner, you must seek counsel and knowledge about money planning to know what is right and true, so that when it is time to put down your idea and to teach others, you have a true, perfect, godly wisdom to give.

We will now go into what I see as financial planning stages.

The first stage is planning from waste. Our waste is often treasure in disguise. Consider all the items you have no need of, in the last year or so – many of these are already waste, and instead of them occupying physical space in your home, let them occupy a space in your bank account. Sell them and keep the money safe in your bank account or give some out to those who need them to enable you to earn the favour of the Lord. Once you have saved the money, take a walk around your district and listen to what people usually complain of, or would take a long walk to get it. List them, and prayerfully seek the face of Lord to know which of these is the right side to cast your investment net, borrowing a leaf from Jesus' advice to His disciples (John 21:6): *And he said unto them, Cast the net on the right side of the ship, and ye shall find. They cast therefore, and now they were not able to draw it for the multitude of fishes.* Convert your knowledge to wealth – don't allow it to lie fallow. Convert your talent to wealth also, to the glory of the Lord. Joseph's gift gave him employment as the number one man in Egypt in his days, to the extent that Joseph would affirm that he was in charge – Genesis 45:8: *So now it was not you that sent me hither, but God: and he hath made me a father to Pharaoh, and lord of all his house, and a ruler throughout all the land of Egypt.* Until now that gift was lying waste in the prison, though he used it to minister to Pharaoh's servant. He was even in the house of Potiphar, who appointed him in charge of his household until Mrs Potiphar seduced him and lied against him, and he was thrown into prison. The same gift in his life was not valued by his brothers, but turned their envy into hatred for him. If you see a gift that is lying wasted in your life, pray to God to use it and announce you. It is possible. With the help of God, my gift in singing, which was lying wasted, is now yielding fruits.

We will now go into your waste bin to find out the amount of food you waste there. This is the source of rodents and insects, and they will create a non-hygienic environment around you. If you can cut down the amount of food you process in your house to only what is needful, you will save from waste already. You will discover that sanitary workers who come to evacuate sanitary pits often complain of greater volume generated from localities where there are more poor people than areas of the rich. What differentiates the rich from the poor is financial planning.

Most rich people would tell you that they were raised in poor homes, or what people will call a humble background. How did they become successful? They simply mingled with enlightened minds, and then discovered where their families made mistakes which they didn't take lessons from. They decide to learn from the failures of yesterday. Our experiences can also be wasted until we are able to employ the lessons learned to better our today and future.

Another source of waste is those whose needs we often cater for. These people can often be very productive, and because of the value society places on some walks of life, many people will just sit down looking for a white-collar job, when they could have been useful in other walks of life. For instance, many people see singing as a hobby and will not devote cost, time and resource to it. I discovered that my singing gift was being wasted. I decided to invest it, and today it is already bearing fruit. I am a successful engineer by all standards. I also pastor – preaching and teaching the word of God - write books, edit videos, produce music and am presently pursuing a higher education qualification to enable me to lecture in the university part-time, so that my wealth of experience will become valuable in the lives of others.

Now that you have identified and planned how to invest the waste and transform it to wealth, I would encourage you to teach others what you have read. In this way, your consciousness will begin to see the subject as a live event that must be given attention to. This will create a spiritual envelope around you to lead you to those who can be of help to you physically, because they will begin to see you as having a value to add to societal growth.

The second stage of financial planning is planning from savings. You should not plan with your after-tax earnings in mind. Rather, set out a certain percentage of your after-tax earnings as savings for further investment – say 30%, then plan with that. This is how you measure how prudent you have become. Take 10% of your income and pay as tithe – it is advisable to bind your job to a spiritual altar, which is very important to ward off all devourers that come in various forms: sickness, accidents, loss of job, armed robbers, car-jacking, loss in investment, swindling, etc. The remaining 60% should be spent on looking after the house, paying school fees, paying utility bills, saving for unforeseen contingencies, care of the less-privileged, etc. You will see now that freezing your savings at 30% will really help you to plan wisely. With your investment ideas in your mind, and having sought the face of God for a direction on how to invest, you may want to start outright, or open an investment savings account, which will only be accessed when the investment opportunity is ripe, with all the necessary considerations already done.

Depending on the kind of investment, you may want to have a personal lawyer. Such a lawyer should be one with a sound economic mind. You may not really need an accountant in the beginning, but ensure there is someone who is knowledgeable enough to address your accounting – credit and debit items. This should do in the beginning.

Now that you have done this, the next tip I would encourage is holistic financial planning from all your earnings. Earlier we fixed a certain percentage for our savings. Now I want you to plan with your entire earnings. Though this is similar to what you did earlier, you will notice that putting everything together will really make you see how each of the items in the plan plays out against the others. From this list, you may even begin to think of increasing your savings to boost your investment purse. You will begin to prioritise better, and see alternative and cheaper ways of meeting some of the items in the list. If you are good at using a Microsoft Excel chart, you can chart your list on a histogram or a pie chart. This you can discuss with your spouse if you are married. As time goes on you can bring in your children, and you will see that you already have a financial planning team right before you, sitting round a table to discuss making money the right way. Every one of the team will see how much space on the chart they are occupying as a result of their financial demands.

This is prudence in action. It works, and it will always work when everyone now has a financial mindset, with the means to reduce finance spending working through everyone's minds. Don't be surprise when your spouse comes to meet you and tell you he or she wants to cut down utility bills by using utilities only when they are needed. You will also notice that the phone bills will drop. If you can involve everyone, it will become everyone's business. Each member of the home will now act as a check on the other – isn't this wonderful?

In all, avoid impulsive buying and living your life on credit. A shopping spree is not a good habit. Health risks like smoking and taking drugs don't save money. Feeding your household with junk foods will only make you a constant customer at the health centre. Expensive weddings and other forms of celebration – including society graduation parties - are money-wasting avenues. The Bible says in Ecclesiastes 5:13: *There is a grievous evil that I have seen under the sun: riches were kept by their owner to his hurt, and those riches were lost in a bad venture.* Nothing is as painful as seeing your hard-earned savings being wasted on items of no economic value. All these – expensive weddings, unnecessary travelling, uncalled-for parties - are bad ventures. The more we indulge in them, the farther away are our days of rest, and we won't have time for God either.

Remember, the money may not always be there to spend. A stitch in time saves nine. Try to cultivate a positive attitude towards all issues – spiritual, social, financial, scientific inventions, war news, sport etc; there may be a financial language which you may not hear at the beginning until you open up your mind to put all the parts together. The information you neglect may be the cornerstone information you would have employed to better your situation.

Insurance cover is good when you are going to have a large investment that will need capital. Seek advice from insurance experts too. You can check on free online tips or blogs on this before engaging insurance personnel. This gives you valuable knowledge that they too can share to put you in the right perspective. The internet is a world of information – take time out to check all you need to know before sailing into the sea of financial planning, instead of wasting precious time on unworthy phone calls and unproductive social networking. There is a time to deep-dive and withdraw for the purpose of thinking and planning, and there is a time to come to the surface to take fresh air, investing your wisdom for the purpose of the physical manifestation of your deep-diving expedition.

Now that we have come this far, I now propose the financial planning cycle below:

Budget – Income – Expenses – Savings – Investment

- **Budget** – This is usually planned from the beginning of the year. A planned yearly budget helps you to know if there is a need for additional investments or to increase your savings in anticipation of a rainy day.

- **Income** – Planned incomes are the incomes we are certain will come over a recurring period such as monthly salary. An average estimation of profits based on historical sales can also become planned income. Unplanned incomes come from profits we make when we suddenly win a contract. This kind of income sometimes, if not well managed, will lead to overblown expenses that may be difficult to bring down for some years ahead. Such windfalls sometimes also give a false estimation of one's financial worth. In all use the base income for planning - all others should go into savings until you are ready to invest.
- **Expenses** – Needs are planned, but our wants may be planned or unplanned. Try to minimise unplanned wants.
- **Savings** – If you have a regular income, then there is the possibility that you will plan a certain percentage of that income as savings. We do also have unplanned income from bumper harvests, special favours and gifts etc. To me this additional increase should go totally as savings after paying your tithes.
- **Investment** – We do have both planned and unplanned investments depending on a lot of factors, including the current political climate, seasonal

demands, natural disasters, etc. Unplanned investments are also termed opportunistic investments. My advice is that all investments must pass through a planning circle where all the issues have been addressed.

CHAPTER TWELVE

TOO MUCH MONEY

There is no way one can have too much money without loving money. This implies that there will definitely be a manifestation of evil in the hearts of many people who have so much money. Acts like lying, arrogance, pride, deceit, and self-centeredness, among other characteristics, may be seen in such a person. So much money breeds arrogance and pride. And since making money has to some extent to do with your ability to see everyone that comes to you as a service provider, you may, unknowingly, reduce the personality of whoever comes across you to that of mere wealth making avenues. Such a person would ask questions like, '*what can I get through this person?*' when they come across them.

Below are some of my thoughts based on what I have seen and read in Scriptures about how too much money has damaged the lives of people.

■ **Serving the devil:** Moses gave a concern that is relevant to our discussion here - Deuteronomy 8:12-14: *Lest when thou hast eaten and art full, and hast built goodly houses, and dwelt therein; And when thy herds and thy flocks multiply, and thy silver and thy gold is multiplied, and all that thou hast is multiplied; Then thine heart be lifted up, and thou forget the Lord thy God.* We may have read in the Bible how King Solomon became an idol worshipper towards the later part of his kingship because with so much wealth, he could afford to have a thousand wives and concubines, and among these were idolaters, and he was led astray to worship their idols. I have examined this event and what I discovered was that while Solomon prayed to be endowed with wisdom, he didn't pray for the power to manage the wealth and fame that wisdom of God was going to give him. I got this from the book of 1 Corinthians 1:24: ... *Christ the power of God, and the wisdom of God.* If he had requested the power of God, he wouldn't have been powerless when his idolatrous wives came with their advances. This would advise: *'what shall it profit a man if he becomes wealthy and loss his soul to the devil?'* The love of money is the worship of mammon. Many millionaires worship the devil and belong to all manner of cults.

- **Negligence of the poor in their midst:** Asaph, a Levite, one of the leaders of David's choir, prayed to the Lord because of the oppression of those in power, who have control of wealth and money, seeing how they oppressed the poor thus - Psalms 74:19-21: ... *forget not the congregation of thy poor for ever. Have respect unto the covenant: for the dark places of the earth are full of the habitations of cruelty. O let not the oppressed return ashamed: let the poor and needy praise thy name.* There is the tendency of trying to use more money to get more, and it will become difficult to spend on others, as you will always want that money to yield physical profit for you rather than the treasure in heaven. When Jesus told the man to sell all he had and give it to the poor, we saw a display of stone-heartedness towards giving – Matthew 19:22: *But when the young man heard that saying, he went away sorrowful: for he had great possessions*, because he know the value of every penny. Those who engage in welfare often do so to attract more customers and recognition and not because they see it as their responsibility before the Lord to provide for the needy, hence they promote the event to the media.

- **Spendthrift living:** One irony I have seen is that because many are from humble backgrounds, they want to spend the money they have now as if trying to make up for the years of financial deprivation they had experienced. Often they don't carry out a good market survey. They want to fly abroad and visit the most expensive markets to buy items, many of which they don't even need. For an ordinary medical check up, they will board a plane abroad. Some have wasted money buying very expensive cars, jet planes and yachts, or celebrate unworthy birthday parties in big hotels that would cost millions of dollars.
- **Arrogance:** Closely related to what we just discussed is arrogance. As wealth increases there is a tendency for many to outstretch their bounds, and see themselves as being on top of the world. They will often not recognise the need to give thanks to God for what they have. There is the tendency of 'self-praise' in every speech they make. This is the character of the devil, and when it starts, we know that downfall is imminent. When this happens many feel they are gods, and want to be worshipped by those they assist. They want to be recognised for whatever they are doing as help to society. Some even lobby

organisations for recognition meant for achievers such as honorary degrees, and use the media to announce this achievement as a feat that is worthy of acclamation. They are seen committing gross social misconduct, and their acts will often deface the image of sainthood they often disguisedly try to portend with the help of the media, as many of them own media outfits too. One clear example of such people was Nebuchadnezzar in the Bible – Daniel 4:30: *The king spake, and said, Is not this great Babylon, that I have built for the house of the kingdom by the might of my power, and for the honour of my majesty.* After this declaration of self-praise, we read further in Daniel 4: 31-37 that a voice from heaven spoke to him, and Nebuchadnezzar lost his senses and lived among animals in the bush until he learnt his lessons and was humbled, when he lifted up his voice to glorify the Lord. King Herod also had this kind of indignation, and he lost his life – Acts 12:1,21-24: *Now about that time Herod the king stretched forth his hands to vex certain of the church. And upon a set day Herod, arrayed in royal apparel, sat upon his throne, and made an oration unto them. And the people gave a shout, saying, It is the voice of a god, and not of a man. And immediately the angel of the Lord smote him, because he gave not God the glory: and he was eaten of worms, and gave up the ghost. But the word of God grew and multiplied.* Many establishments have been visited with the wrath of God, because the owners had seen themselves as gods.

- **Undermining the respect for the dignity of man:** It is the belief of many that once you reduce the value of everybody around you to what they can provide and an avenue for making wealth, you are on your way to ruling the world. Many of those who swim in much money become filled with the impression of being above the law. People working under many such people work under duress. They make them work for their salary so to speak – even when they are stressed. We are admonished in Luke 14:11: *For whosoever exalteth himself shall be abased; and he that humbleth himself shall be exalted.* Romans 12:10 also advises - *Be kindly affectioned one to another with brotherly love; in honour preferring one another.* Let not money change this character of heaven in us. The poor often seem to be helpless although they have the knowledge of where the wealth in most localities is stored. They are the first to report an occurrence, for instance, oil spilling from the ground or a shining rock in their farm, to the rulers, who would in some cases engage the services of experts to find out if what the poor saw could yield money. The poor are also those who mostly have their money saved in banks in the hope of getting interest on their savings. The rich man comes and takes this money, sets up an establishment and employs the poor to work, and if the establishment can provide health care, housing, and a basic holiday retreat for the poor, it is a done deal – the poor will labour through the hours of the day and night to make the rich laugh all the way to the bank.

- **Create more waste:** So much money in the hand makes many spend lots of money on wants, instead of using it for their needs. Many have cars they don't drive occupying their garages, houses they don't live in and wouldn't rent out – they are seldom kept for their many sex-mad guests, designer fashions which are branded with their names, and flocking with the high class in society wasting money in unnecessary celebrations all in the name of the idea that 'money is meant to be spent.' Many have also become drug addicts, and have lots of evil people around them whom they use to secure authority and power to influence by force in society. They also incur unnecessary interest on avoidable loans. I once came across a millionaire trying to take what he termed a 'soft loan' to enable him to spend on a friend's daughter's wedding. In project terms, operating expenditure (OPEX) is treated as 'sunk expenses,' because they cannot be recovered back 100% - this is the same with most items people waste money on. Capital expenditure (CAPEX) on the other hand still retains its value 100%, and could serve the same purpose and may even go up in value, depending on market factors such as inflation. So much money creates waste when the excess money is employed to serve OPEX purposes, such as we have been discussing since. In effect what makes people poor is when their OPEX exceeds the revenue that their CAPEX can generate.

- **Create aristocratic tendencies:** The high class take over society, having so much money in their hands. They take over the government through hijacking the polls in most countries. They also sponsor military coups d'état and sponsor religious wars. They want to become household names and romance those in the corridors of power, so that they can always have their way. So much money creates class. We have heard of Government Reservation Areas (GRAs) and other high-class housing estates. They own life in the city – casinos, hotels, clubhouses, etc. They pay for expensive wine and brandy. And most cases, the poor have no face where they are present.

- **Greed:** Closely related to what we have discussed above is their desire to influence government decisions to achieve personal gain, while undermining the larger populace. They lobby governments to make laws that would ban the importation of certain products, thereby forcing their low quality products on the populace, which may seem to be cheaper, but are actually more expensive from the quality perspective. There is the possibility of economic monopoly, oligopoly and monopsony – the rich offer a price that no other would cope with, and then control the market. They steal by tricks – bid for a contract with low cost and come back for a variation to be able to make a certain margin of profit. Many give bribes and also take bribes, just to ensure they get what they want. The Bible warns (Leviticus 19:35,36): *Ye shall do no unrighteousness in judgment, in meteyard, in weight, or in measure. Just balances, just weights, a just ephah, and a just hin, shall ye have: I am the Lord your God, which brought you out of the land of Egypt.*
- **Brings stone-heartedness:** This is however an inherent spirit that leads to what we have been discussing above, but here I am talking about non-readiness to take good advice that will make them godly, and have mercy on others.

- **Deception and oppression:** They don't allow others to air their concerns and voice - imposing decisions on people. Even the mega IT companies like Microsoft, Apple etc impose new products on customers through the use of mind-manipulating adverts. Others trying to enter the market are deprived of a good market share because they don't have what it takes to push their products across the media. Through the use of a media-agenda-setting philosophy, it is possible that the big weights will push products of even lesser value than their cost into the market. They showcase their products in sports stadia because they have the money to sponsor sports programmes. There have been cases of deceptive adverts all over the world. And because they really don't want their advice to fall to the ground, they tend to use money to buy support for their ill and selfish opinions.
- **Promiscuity and crime:** Immorality and crime is bred by the use of money, which means that more money in the hands of people means more immorality and more crime. For instance the high-class prostitutes who sleep with multimillionaires have been seen with expensive houses and cars. The Bible says in Leviticus 19:29: *Do not prostitute thy daughter, to cause her to*

be a whore; lest the land fall to whoredom, and the land become full of wickedness. Prostitution in any land leads to wickedness. This is one reason why those in the corridors of power who are promiscuous care less about the plight of the people.

- **Mental stress:** If there is one thing too much money can take from anybody, it is sleep. Having sleepless nights is a common occurrence occasioned by more financial assistance demands, more security needs, including riding in bulletproof cars, care for the 'boys' and more social names such as chieftaincy titles, honorary degrees, national awards etc to maintain. While many try to become philanthropists, they can hardly cope with the occasional outburst of anger that stares at their faces as they try to please everybody that comes their way.
- **Bringing about war:** As the rich protect their business empires and want more market share, there is the tendency to try to run down other business owners, and in most developing countries, the rich, who have the wherewithal to buy firearms, also sponsor wars. As many also invest in solid minerals so also their quest for control makes them to think of eliminating others, and as they spend money for the 'boys' in the streets who

have been neglected by the government this will buy their loyalty. Soon these big weights will use these boys to start a rebel fight, which will finally grow into war.

- **Dubious bank owners:** They own banks and use them to defraud the public, when they are certain that they can't get loans from other banks, maybe due to political differences. Many failed banks in Nigeria were owned by such people. The money stored in their banks is taken at lower or no interest rates and used to finance contracts, especially government projects. They will often not complete the contracts and not pay back the loans, yet still collect the value of the contract if not more.
- **Inability to raise their children with good morals:** While in the university, I have heard many cultists affirming that their parents advised them to study law and also join a cult, so that they could be used to hanker after their parents' wealth. More money means more absence from the home, and often leads to growing and bringing up children with nannies and house helps, many of whom will train them in the ill characteristics they later grow up with.
- **Isolation:** A time always comes when those with too much money start to avoid people, even keeping away

from their very close allies. This happens when they feel they have stepped on too many toes, and may have received threat letters from all the people they had associated with in their money-making ventures, including prostitutes who want to blackmail them to make cheap money. There is also this belief that they are being hunted. Then many will return to God for protection, and often want quick spiritual solutions. This desire often lands them in the hands of fake prophets or cultists, who would bind their souls to the devil's coven. Soon, all the wealth will be gone while they are still alive, or after they are dead. Others will hand over their properties for the work of God, but be too frail to accept that their sins have been forgiven.

All those things we have been talking about are manifestations of the spirit of mammon.

CHAPTER THIRTEEN

STRIVING DURING FAMINE

Is there not enough famine in the world already? The more we listen to the news around the world, the more we know that it is already experiencing gradual desolation and famine. If the Lord is angry, the world can go through a dearth and sorrowful events – Jeremiah 14:12: *When they fast, I will not hear their cry; and when they offer burnt offering and an oblation, I will not accept them: but I will consume them by the sword, and by the famine, and by the pestilence.*

When famine becomes inevitable, it is advisable to seek ways to cope during the period. Can God provide for His own; those who favour His righteous course during famine? Yes He can and does provide! We would be taking a story from Elijah's days – he cursed the land not to receive dew and rain because they neglected the service of the Lord – while God answered and sent no dew nor rain into the land, and famine struck the land, God still provided for Elijah – 1 Kings 17:6-9: *And the ravens brought him bread and flesh in the morning, and bread and flesh in the evening; and he drank of the brook. And it came to pass after a while, that the brook dried up, because there had been no rain in the land. And the word of the Lord came unto him, saying, Arise, get thee to Zarephath, which belongeth to Zidon, and dwell there: behold, I have commanded a widow woman there to sustain thee.* Our hope therefore in famine is sustained in the Lord. We would now, in this session, see how this could be.

Will there be famine? I got a word from the immortal realm some time in 2013. I didn't take it seriously, but as events happening around the world prove now, it has dawned on me that it could just be true and caution should be taken. In that revelation, I saw a hot rolling wind coming from the desert and sweeping across lands – and whichever land it crossed, everything there died. The hot rolling wind is war, and associated with war is pestilence and famine. And today we have war coming from the deserts and sweeping across lands. The recent Islamic insurgence, ISIS, attacks and airstrikes are an indication of the sweeping wind from the desert. When I look at the acronym for the Islamic States in Iraq and Syria, ISIS it reminds me of the Egyptian Isis - goddess of health, marriage, love, and of the underworld. With the powers of the underworld manipulating humans to destroy their neighbours, it won't be long before famine strikes. Another possible source of famine is climate change, and it is the first item on the long list of issues addressed at the 2014 United Nations General Assembly in New York. From the Bible it has been proven that famine is sent as punishment by God to win the heart of the world back to Him after they had gone after idols to serve and worship them – Ezekiel 5:16: *When I shall send upon them the evil arrows of famine, which shall be for their destruction, and which I will send to destroy you: and I will increase the famine upon you, and will break your staff of bread.* This looming famine is as a result of the increasing sin in the world today. Matthew 24:7 also say - *For nation shall rise against nation, and kingdom against kingdom: and there shall be famines, and pestilences, and earthquakes, in divers places. All these are the beginning of sorrows*

Extreme cases of famine could lead to the following:

- Deprivation of food as many would become cannibals: Those who have experienced civil wars will confirm this – Deuteronomy 28:53: *And thou shalt eat the fruit of thine own body, the flesh of thy sons and of thy daughters.* Jeremiah 48:33: *And joy and gladness is taken from the plentiful field, and from the land of Moab; and I have caused wine to fail from the winepresses: none shall tread with shouting; their shouting shall be no shouting.* Lamentation 1:11: *All her people sigh, they seek bread; they have given their pleasant things for meat to relieve the soul*
- Driven into captivity: We have many today running from one nation to another in search of greener pastures. Some, especially in Nigeria, have decided to have children abroad, especially in the US, so that their children can become US citizens, because they have lost hope in the future of their homeland. The Bible says in Isaiah 5:13: *Therefore my people are gone into captivity, because they have no knowledge: and their honourable men are famished, and their multitude dried up with thirst.*
- Increasing acts of wickedness in the land, as many become deprived of their properties by the ruling

class, and in some cases, high taxes would lead to more poverty – Isaiah 9:18 -19: *For wickedness burneth as the fire: it shall devour ... and the people shall be as the fuel of the fire: no man shall spare his brother.*

- Poor harvest from the farmlands, as great heat in the land burns the plants and cause them to rot, and decreases returns from business – Isaiah 17:11: *In the day shalt thou make thy plant to grow, and in the morning shalt thou make thy seed to flourish: but the harvest shall be a heap in the day of grief and of desperate sorrow.* Joel 1:17: *The seed is rotten under their clods, the garners are laid desolate, the barns are broken down; for the corn is withered.*
- An increasing mortality and morbidity rate in the land as a result of malnutrition and lack of water – Jeremiah 14:1-3: *The word of the Lord that came to Jeremiah concerning the dearth. Judah mourneth, and the gates thereof languish; they are black unto the ground; and the cry of Jerusalem is gone up. And their nobles have sent their little ones to the waters: they came to the pits, and found no water.*
- Loss of dignity and honour, and rejection by many – Lamentation 1:19: *I called for my lovers, but they deceived me: my priests and mine elders gave up the*

ghost in the city, while they sought their meat to relieve their souls.

- Sorrow and tears all over the land as people see the deaths of children placating the land, and young women being sold out into marriage by their hungry parents – Lamentations 2:11: *Mine eyes do fail with tears, my bowels are troubled, my liver is poured upon the earth, for the destruction of the daughter of my people; because the children and the sucklings swoon in the streets of the city.*

How could one cope in the midst of famine? The solution lies in the words of Jesus in what we now call the Lord's Prayer – Matthew 6:9-13: *Our Father which art in heaven, Hallowed be thy name. Thy kingdom come. Thy will be done in earth, as it is in heaven. Give us this day our daily bread. And forgive us our debts, as we forgive our debtors. And lead us not into temptation, but deliver us from evil: For thine is the kingdom, and the power, and the glory, for ever. Amen.*

Now we would get all we need to do spiritually, out:

We should continually seek the face of the Lord.

We should always worship and praise the Lord.

We should expect the end of the famine and therefore pray for the famine to end - *thy kingdom come.*

We must continually seek repentance as a way of doing the Will of God on earth.

We should seek daily bread only in order not to wear ourselves out with unnecessary hope for more, while we fast more and pray more.

We should keep on asking for forgiveness because we are mere imperfect souls in a mortal body.

Forgive others, and preach love and unity, to be able to attract the favour of the Lord, and be able to help one another during the famine.

Pray against war, pestilence, and temptation.

Pray to be delivered from the evil that comes through temptation – stealing, promiscuity, covetousness, deceit, swindling.

Submit to the Will and Power of God, and give him thanks for all that happens and would ever happen to us.

Let nothing separate us from the Lord, no matter what happens – Romans 8:35: *Who shall separate us from the love of Christ? shall tribulation, or distress, or persecution, or famine, or nakedness, or peril, or sword.*

Now that we have addressed the spiritual side of what we should do during famine, we need to also discuss what we should have done and will do physically:

Save money before the famine, so that you are able to invest in properties that would be sold during the period. This was how Jeremiah bought his land – Jeremiah 32:9-10: *And I bought the field of Hanameel my uncle's son, that was in Anathoth, and weighed him the money, even seventeen shekels of silver. And I subscribed the evidence, and sealed it, and took witnesses, and weighed him the money in the balances.* Even Joseph made Pharaoh richer this way – Genesis 47:20: *And Joseph bought all the land of Egypt for Pharaoh; for the Egyptians sold every man his field, because the famine prevailed over them: so the land became Pharaoh's.* This was why, when the Israelites where suffering, it was obvious that the new Pharaoh didn't know the works of Joseph – Exodus 1:8: *Now there arose up a new king over Egypt, which knew not Joseph.* If Joseph had made his people rich in their original land without bringing them into Egypt, the Israelites wouldn't have had the need for fight to reclaim the land after 430 years of sojourn in Egypt. This was the prophecy of the Lord to Abraham (Genesis 15:13): *And he said unto Abram, Know of a surety that thy seed shall be a stranger in a land that is not theirs, and shall serve them; and they shall afflict them four hundred years.* Why would a loving God send the descendants of His servant into a land where they would be treated as slaves? It is a mystery that only God has answers to and I believe it was done to set the path for the salvation of the world – because Egypt was the first civilization the world ever had, and a centre of world tourism and trade. This is also why the Lord can visit the earth at will with famine. The children of Israel ended up staying as sojourners in the land of Egypt for 430 years – Exodus 12:40: *Now the sojourning of the children of Israel, who dwelt in Egypt, was four hundred and thirty years.* Now from above, after 390 years, Moses started the rescue by killing the first Egyptian, but for fear of being persecuted, he ran away and stayed 40 years outside Egypt, until God sent him back. If this was not so, their sorrow would have ended after exactly 400 years. This is also learning for us, even in the midst of famine, to be steadfast in the Lord and to support those He is raising to help us learn His ways, else the famine period may extend more than necessary.

- Be educated in multiple professions, as I said earlier. Even in the midst of famine, learn what you can, morally, spiritually, professionally, so that you are always relevant as the tide shifts. This is a time to be helpful in voluntary care services as many would be sick and hungry-looking. It is a time to lend a helping hand, and your education can be of real help, especially in the medical vocation. Good understanding of modern sophisticated agricultural practice would also be of help, so that we would still have food, even if in small quantities. This a time to serve as Dorcas did – Acts 9:39 … *and all the widows stood by him weeping, and shewing the coats and garments which Dorcas made…*

- Belong to a community of believers to be able to partake in the available relief provisions sent to the church – Acts 11:29: *Then the disciples, every man according to his ability, determined to send relief unto the brethren which dwelt in Judaea.* This is the time to build relationships and keep them. World record figures available from the Internal Displacement Monitoring Centre (IDMC)[3], as at the 22nd of September 2014 show that globally, 22 million people were displaced by natural disasters such as floods, storms and earthquakes in 2013 alone and 33.3 million people displaced by conflicts, including those displaced by the

Islamist group Boko Haram in Nigeria, from 2010, as of January 2014. With global climate change, there is the tendency for multiple famines that may be experienced across the globe. This places a concern on us all.

- Move into a smaller apartment before the famine if you are in a rented apartment and your income cannot sustain you.
- Reduce the number of cars in your garage. Go for low fuel consumption cars, and learn to plan your movement, for there is joy in walking. Don't drive on impulse – plan every movement.
- Avoid trouble, so that you won't have a case in the law court, or have people hunting you.

Benefits of famine include:

- Humility.
- Learning to wait on the Lord.
- Better ways of making savings.
- Invention of better ways of farming. The majority of modern agricultural practices came out of famine, as men began to think better.

- Improvement in storage and preservation technology. For instance, the building of grain silos was prompted by the need to preserve foods for a rainy day.
- Birth control practices.
- In some cases it could unite families who have lived in enmity.

It is our hope that the Lord shall redeem His own during famine, and we have the promise of the Lord to this fact:

Job 5:20: *In famine he shall redeem thee from death: and in war from the power of the sword*

Psalm 33:19: *To deliver their soul from death, and to keep them alive in famine. Our soul waiteth for the Lord: he is our help and our shield*

Psalm 37:19: *They shall not be ashamed in the evil time: and in the days of famine they shall be satisfied*

CHAPTER FOURTEEN

SAVE YOUR TOMORROW TODAY

In this chapter we will summarise all we have been discussing since the beginning of this knowledge and wisdom-seeking journey. It is time to move into tomorrow today and ensure that our tomorrow doesn't die today. To save our tomorrow today, we need to understand how to sow both physical and spiritual seeds, so that they will begin to complement each other. When your physical seeds are drying up, your spiritual seeds will send forth fruits of righteousness unto the realm of the Lord, for Him to send down rains of favour upon your physical seed. They will then grow into giant trees of honour for everyone to behold, bearing fruits of righteousness which will establish you as the apple of God's eye, and the planting of the Lord – Isaiah 61:3: *To appoint unto them that mourn in Zion, to give unto them beauty for ashes, the oil of joy for mourning, the garment of praise for the spirit of heaviness; that they might be called trees of righteousness, the planting of the Lord, that he might be glorified.*

- The Breath of God on your investment: God breathed on Adam, Jesus also did on His disciples. Once the Holy Ghost enveloped Mary, she conceived. If your investment has the breath of God, it won't die.
- Cast out the Devourer on time, right from the onset, by submitting and remaining loyal to the commandments of God.
- Build good neighbourliness – Proverbs 27:10: *Thine own friend, and thy father's friend, forsake not; neither go into thy brother's house in the day of thy calamity: for better is a neighbour that is near than a brother far off.* Proverbs 25:21 also says - *If thine enemy be hungry, give him bread to eat; and if he be thirsty, give him water to drink.*
- Avoid wasting in advance – wasting others' finance is like sowing a seed of your own wastage for the future.

- Water your investment: Watering requires getting the right water. Don't eat all your profits. Be relevant. Understand good marketing skills.
- Have a five-year saving and expenses plan – get the right education, open accounts in the bank, plan your retirement.
- Save for a rainy day - you never can tell.
- Have enough only for the weekend by practising the 'manna' principle. Too much money over the weekend breeds an avenue for waste.
- Marry a prudent spouse. Do not marry a spendthrift – Provides 19:14… *a prudent wife is from the Lord.*

The reason many of us are unable to serve God is the chasing of money. A lack of financial planning will not allow you to settle down early in life, and especially to get married. When we chase money we begin to tell lies and commit other sins, then we create holes in our investments for the devourer to take its course.

Be the better for what you live to achieve on Earth.

Shalom!

COVENANT CONFESSION

If you are not born again, you may have read this book as literary material and will not receive the spirit it carries. You can make a decision to correct that now by saying this covenant confession:

Lord Jesus, I know now that you died for my sins. I believe and confess you as my Lord and Saviour. Please come into my life and dwell inside me.

If you just said this confession, you should locate a spirit-filled church to join in fellowship with them – let the pastor know you just gave your life to Christ and you will be directed on what to do next. Salvation is a personal race and you must be serious with it.

You can also call us through the numbers below: +234-8076190064; +234-8086737791. Or send us an email at: christmovementinternational@gmail.com

OTHER BOOKS BY THE SAME AUTHOR

Existing In The Supernatural

The Altar In Golgotha

How Good and Large is your Land?

Born To Blossom

Battles Beyond The Physical

The Path To Absolute Freedom

The Man God Made

Aspects of Marriage

Leadership – An Eagle-Eye Perspective

Gifted and Anointed

The Subject of Love – A Discourse

The Mystery Of The Kingdom Of God On Earth

Understand Your Destiny

The Nonsense of War

ABOUT THE AUTHOR

Pastor Oghenethoja Umuteme encountered God the day he was baptised at St Stephen's Anglican Church, Owhelogbo Delta State, when he received a warm feeling in his heart as he confessed the Lord Jesus as His lord and personal saviour. His birth was surrounded with mysteries – he was born to a mother who had been barren for eight years. There was hardly anything he said that did not come to pass as he was growing. In 1994 he had a dream in which he received an orange which contained a bible with a red cover. Events continued dramatically until he started hearing voices telling him to go for rescue, as many souls were heading for destruction. Then it became clear to him that he was being called to carry out the task of restoring mankind back to Jesus.

In January 2006, he heard a voice telling him to read Isaiah 42. On reading to verse 6, he felt a deep force within him and started trembling and a voice said - 'I have called you'. As he read further he was getting immersed in the spirit of God and when he read verse 22, the voice said, 'this is your task'. Then on the 13th of October 2008, he heard a voice while driving: 'Service starts in your house on Sunday.' Events happened that were beyond his understanding and on Sunday 19th October 2008, the first public worship service came to pass.

Pastor Oghenethoja Umuteme is a prolific writer and oversees a leadership foundation, Umuteme Leadership Foundation, which he uses to teach good leadership and a School of Ministry to empower church leaders. A member of the Nigerian Society of Engineers, he has eleven years' work experience in the oil and gas industry in different pipeline engineering functions – design, procurement, fabrication, construction, integrity management, maintenance and operation. A gospel musician with two recorded album, *Breaking Through* and *Smile Again*, he is also the Founder and Senior Pastor at Royal Diamonds International Church, Port Harcourt, Nigeria. He is an established teacher of the word of God and a prophet to the nation, as shown by his books. Using his crusade ministry, Giant Strides World Outreach Crusade, Pst. Oghenethoja reaches people with the undiluted word of salvation. And as a prophet to the nations, he has declared prophecies that have been fulfilled – the latest one being the famine that will visit the earth for ten years starting from the year 2017 and ending in 2027. He is also a man of miracles with testimonies said by those who have benefited from the gift of God in his life. As a motivational preacher, he has encouraged many to become successful in their chosen careers. The books God has used him to write have brought healing and encouraged many all over the world with testimonies. Many, including pastors, have also used these books as teaching and counselling materials. A time with him is a time filled with wisdom, joy and humour. He is often referred to as *'primus inter pares.'* His wife, Mrs. Umuteme Adokiye Obele, who supports him in this call of God upon his life, has borne him children.

[1] http://www.bls.gov/news.release/pdf/cesan.pdf

[2] Oghenethoja Umuteme: How good and Large is your land – 2014, Restoration Media House Ltd, Port Harcourt, Nigeria

[3] http://www.internal-displacement.org

www.ingramcontent.com/pod-product-compliance
Lightning Source LLC
LaVergne TN
LVHW051629080426
835511LV00016B/2249
9781909874831